"This is an excellent book on apologetics. I appreciated the author's research and his clear, concise points."

"The beauty of this book is that it does seek objective truth, and arms those of faith with weapons to defend their beliefs.‖

"Loved it, I would recommend this book to anyone who has serious questions about Christianity and how it applies to all of us."

—I was given a copy by a friend about two years ago when I told them I didn't believe but had an encounter with what I now know was the Holy Spirit prior to reading the book. After reading your book, and being that I'm a cop, the evidence was compelling, so the choice became easy. Thank you for being a big part of saving my life and seeing the truth about Jesus. My life has drastically changed for the better!!!‖

–I've now recommended and used your books extensively in my ministry at Oklahoma State University. My whole ministry team is using these and handing them out. We've had at least four people we can name who have come to faith in Christ as a direct result of reading the book.‖

–Your book continues to be a big hit with the inmates. I love how a well written and thought out apologetic can take away a person's intellectual excuses. Then they are faced with the truth of the gospel and what Jesus has done for each of us. This is what your book accomplishes and does it well. I've found old tattered copies of your book with inmate's signatures in the back with the dates they made commitments to follow Christ.‖

 –Just read your book for the second time and thought I would check out your website. Thank you for writing the book and opening my eyes. I thoroughly enjoyed it and appreciate what you have done. It was just what I was looking for.‖

Gravity - True For You But Not For Me

Evidence for God's Existence and Identity

Michael Edwards

Thank you to Beate, who always keeps God first. Without her help, this book would have never been written.

Table of Contents

Dear Friend, can you imagine jumping off the edge of a high cliff without a parachute while screaming, "Gravity is true for you but not for me!" Not unless you're crazy, right? We all know the law of gravity is true because of the evidence. We drop something and it falls, we trip and we fall. I like to point out to people that my dogs have no idea what gravity is, so they can't believe in it, but they never float away. Gravity is true for everyone, believe it or not.

But do you think that any single belief about God can be true for everyone? I have often heard people say, "God is true for you, but something else is true for me," as if the truth about God is just personal opinion. In fact, the Bible claims to be true for everyone, whether they believe it or not, just like gravity. In essence, it warns that leaving this world without heeding the Bible's crucial advice is more foolish than jumping out of a plane without a parachute.

It's certain that you have some thoughts about God's existence or non-existence. The question is—do you have any objective evidence to back it up? If not, no matter what you believe, it's blind faith. If your belief is founded on your feelings or based on what someone else believes, you are in for a surprise. The truth about God's existence and identity has nothing to do with feelings or what any person or group desires to be true. Truth is discovered, not invented.

If you have ever thought your family or friends want you to become a Christian simply because they want you to believe what they believe, you are mistaken. They want you to believe because the evidence suggests it's true.

The person who gave you this book cares about you. He or she believes that you deserve a chance to examine the facts with your own eyes and be aware of the Bible's implications for your life, now and for eternity. This book is not an attempt to try to force you to believe what Christians believe. Nor does it suggest that you commit intellectual suicide to believe in God. It contains sound facts and encourages you to use reason, logic, and common sense to make an informed decision. The Christian faith has a tremendous foundation of scientific and historical support that no other religious belief can claim. These facts are often distorted and ignored by a popular culture which would prefer it to be false.

"Christianity, if false, is of no importance, and if true, of infinite importance. The only thing it cannot be is moderately important." – God in the Dock, C. S. Lewis.

Inside, you will find an easy-to-read basic outline of the evidence. Stick with me, as we begin with the fundamentals to determine if truth exists, what it is and what it is not. Understanding how truth really works is crucial for discovering the truth about God and the purpose of life, so please pay close attention.

"Is life a glorified monopoly game? When you die, does everything just go back in the box?" Dr. Frank Turek, author and speaker, I Don't Have Enough Faith to Be an Atheist. www.crossexamined.org

It is not about religion, it's about truth.

Truth - Is Truth Important to You?

• If you were dying of a deadly but curable disease, would you want the right medication to survive?

• Would you want to know the truth about the risks before investing your life savings?

• Do you want your family and friends to tell you the truth once in a while, or all of the time?

• If you were charged with a murder you did not commit, would you want the truth to come out?

If you want truth in these areas, it appears that truth really is important to you. So, what's on the other side of death? If God exists and your destination after physical death is based on the choices you make in this life, would the truth about eternity be important?

What is Objective Truth?

• It relates to the object referred to.

• It corresponds with reality.

• It is telling it like it is.

• It is true even if no one believes it.

—Truth is true—even if no one knows it. Truth is true—even if no one admits it. Truth is true—even if no one agrees what it is. Truth is true—even if no one follows it. Truth is true—even if no one but God grasps it fully.‖ Paul Copan, Chair of Philosophy and Ethics at Palm Beach Atlantic University, author, True For You But Not For Me.

—Truth is incontrovertible. Malice may attack it and ignorance may deride it, but, in the end, there it is.‖ Sir Winston Churchill, www.quotations.about.com

What is The Law of Non-Contradiction?

The law of non-contradiction is our built-in lie detector to help us find truth. It is a fundamental principle of thought which clearly tells us that opposite ideas cannot both be true at the same time and in the same sense. For example, the earth cannot be flat and sphere-shaped at the same time. The law of non-contradiction is self-evident and undeniable. Knowledge of this law is crucial to understanding that truth does exist and its opposite is always false.

It's true that you are reading this book right now. You are the object in this statement. So it's true for everybody, everywhere that you are reading this book right now. It's a contradiction, or false, that you are not reading it. Since it's true that Washington D.C. is the capital of the United States of America, any other belief, even the next closest city geographically, is contradictory and false. You have particular first and last names that are true, while any other names are false. We all took multiple choice tests in school; one answer was true while the rest were false, no matter how close to the truth they came. Truth is always narrow and exclusive, excluding its opposites.

Conclusion – Truth exists, it's important, and its contradictions are always false.

What is The Best Way to Find Truth?

I am sure you will agree that a person can stumble into truth. We all guessed correctly on a few school tests. But guessing or hoping to find the truth by mere accident is obviously not the best way to make an important decision. The following are three popular ways people use to conclude that something is true.

1. My feelings—it feels right and it gives me purpose, hope and peace of mind, so I believe it's the truth.

2. My family or someone I trust believes it, so I do.

3. Evidence, consistency, best fit to the evidence.

Which one of the three would you select as the best way to discover truth when you had to make an important decision?

Ninety-five percent of the hundreds of people I have asked this question, choose the third option right away. Chances are you chose number three too. That is exactly what this book is about, objective evidence that leads to an informed decision and thus reasonable faith.

Conclusion – The best way to discover truth is by examining the objective evidence.

Can Sincere Faith Make a Belief True?

Many people think that faith is about believing something strongly enough (especially about God) so it will come true. They believe faith is more important than what they place their faith in, but they are mistaken.

The truth is—the object of a person's faith is much more important than the faith itself.

Here is an example. We are going skydiving and I offer you a parachute or a contraption I made in my garage last night. Which one would you pick? I would hope you'd pick the parachute, because there is no evidence that my contraption works. Faith based on evidence is reasonable faith. In this example, the parachute and my contraption are the objects. If faith is more important than the object, you could strap anything on your back and jump out of the plane, but that's not realistic. For faith to ultimately work, it must be placed in truth. To find which option has the highest probability of being true, we need evidence. If you had picked my contraption, you would be exercising blind faith.

So, why would we rely on blind faith to make one of the most important decisions in our lives—God's existence and identity and our eternity? It only makes sense to check out the facts to see if our belief is supported by evidence. When you consider a detective who solves mysteries for a living, it's clear that if he never examines the facts, or if he files criminal charges based on feelings or what someone else believes, he would most likely come to a faulty conclusion.

To give you a mental picture of what we will be doing, let's imagine that you wanted to walk across the ice to the other side of a frozen lake. Before you placed your faith in the ice, you would want some evidence that it would support you, because thin ice could lead to death. You might ask questions of the locals and look to see if anyone was out on the ice. You might cut a hole in the ice and check the thickness. But since it's not possible to be one hundred percent certain the ice will support you all the way across the lake, there would come a point where you would need to exercise faith—making a decision based upon what you did know—if you ever hoped to get to the other side. In our investigation, we will follow the evidence as far as it will take us; faith will be required to make the rest of the journey. That sounds more reasonable than blindly running out onto thin ice, doesn't it?

The Merriam Webster Dictionary defines faith as ―A firm belief in something for which there is no proof,‖ but it does not say ―for which there is no evidence.‖ http://www.merriam-webster.com/dictionary/faith

Faith is very important and is required for any decision where we do not have one hundred percent proof; therefore, it is essential to Christianity. It is also required for those who claim God does not exist, since no one observed the beginning of the universe, first life or the evolution of one species/kind into another as some claim happened.

When it comes to Christianity, the Bible states that faith connects us to the salvation God is offering through grace. Therefore, without faith, a person cannot place their trust in God for salvation. But the Bible is speaking about faith placed in the truth, which it claims to be. Even the most sincere faith will not make my contraption perform like a parachute or make the ice thicker. It cannot change history (if Jesus did not rise from the dead, even sincere faith will not change that fact) and it will not make a false

9

belief about God true. While I know we could find adults who believe in the Greek gods Zeus and Apollo, if they aren't real, not even sincere faith will make them true.

Conclusion – The object of faith is more important than faith. If the object is false, even sincere faith will not make it true.

True for You But Not for Me

The statement true for you but not for me has a long list of problems that tell us it is false. I bring it up because people sometimes claim that —Christianity is true for you but not for me.‖ People who make this statement have confused belief with truth. But belief alone does not guarantee that the matter at hand is true. Truth, on the other hand, is not a respecter of any belief that contradicts it. Truth conforms to reality and the object being referred to. The title of this book is a contradiction on purpose to get your attention: Gravity—True For You But Not For Me. It suggests that an objective truth like gravity does not apply to a person who does not believe in it. But since this is simply not how truth works, the title of this book is just as self-defeating as the claim, —The Bible is true for you but something else is true for me.‖ The following quote reveals an easy way to prove this for yourself:

—True for you but not for me is a self-defeating and therefore false statement. You can prove this one conclusively to yourself today, just drive 90 in a 55 and when the cop stops you for speeding, just say, ‗That's true for you but not for me,' and speed off. Since it's not true for you he can't give you a ticket, right?‖ Dr. Frank Turek author and speaker, www.Crossexamined.org

True for you but not for me also claims that everything is true as long as someone believes it. If that's the case, we should have all received perfect grades in school. Every answer I gave was true—for me.

If God does not exist, this would be true for everyone, everywhere if they believe it or not. However, if God exists and the Bible is true, this is true for everyone, everywhere, if they believe it or not. The only way to make a reasonable decision is to investigate the evidence.

Why Everyone's Belief About God Cannot Be True

Many sincere and good people who have varying beliefs about God have the right to believe whatever they want. However, everyone's belief cannot be true when it comes to God's existence and identity. This is not uncaring or intolerant; it's simply how truth works. If truth could contradict itself, a Christian and an atheist would both be correct about God's existence; we know this is impossible.

Suppose you were a detective and six people showed up (an atheist, a Buddhist, a Muslim, a Mormon, a Hindu and a Christian) with different stories, all claiming to be the sole heir of a tremendous fortune. Could they all be telling the truth? No, you would immediately recognize the obvious problem. Six people claiming to be the sole heir is a contradiction and could not possibly be true. Therefore, you would check out their stories and follow the evidence to uncover the truth. At some point, their explanations would be contradictory to the facts in your investigation. Once you discover who the actual heir is, you would know for certain that the other five claims were false, no matter how close to the truth they appeared.

When it comes to God, we have a similar situation. Many people have shown up who claim to know the truth about God. On the surface, it may seem as if most of them are headed in the same direction. But when we look closely, we see that they all contradict each other when it comes to the most important points, like salvation. For example, Christianity is the sole belief that teaches salvation by God's grace, through faith alone. The others teach

11

works (good deeds) and specific conditions as a necessity. It is also the sole belief that teaches Jesus was God in the flesh who came to save us. The others teach that Jesus was not God.

Contradictory Claims About Jesus, Salvation and Eternity

1. Biblical Christianity – One God, Jesus the Son is God in the flesh; salvation by God's grace through faith in Jesus alone; heaven for believers; non-believers end up in hell.

2. Traditional Roman Catholicism – One God, Jesus the Son is God in the flesh; salvation by God's grace through faith in Jesus plus works, sacraments and penance here and in purgatory; heaven is the end result for true believers; non- believers in hell. (Many Catholics would agree with the points listed under number one. Number two is traditional Catholicism.)

3. Judaism – One God; beliefs about Jesus vary from great moral teacher to idol to a false prophet; just a man not the Messiah/Savior they believe is still to come; Jewish believers can sanctify their lives and draw closer to God by obeying divine commandments and doing good works; God will reward the good and punish the wicked; the dead will be resurrected; extreme evildoers like Hitler to eternal punishment.

4. Islam – Jesus was a prophet; salvation by belief in Allah, Mohammad and good works; true believers go to heaven; non-Muslims in hell.

5. Hinduism – Jesus was a prophet; millions of gods; salvation through good works and overcoming karma; reincarnation.

6. Buddhism – Jesus was an enlightened man; salvation by the cessation of desire through eight-fold path and works; extinguish the ego to enter nirvana, a form of heaven. Buddha was a raised Hindu and rejected Hinduism and god, because of the caste

system. Some claim he was an atheist. Some later forms of Buddhism have added god in some form to their teaching.

7. Higher Power – Whatever anyone believes about God, Jesus, salvation and eternity are true. Every belief about God is true as long as someone believes it. (Embracing all teachings as equally true teaches that truth can contradict itself, which we know is false.)

8. New Age – Jesus was an enlightened man/god; salvation not needed because we are all gods like Jesus, but don't realize it; reincarnation in new life based on works; contradictions among adherents embraced so beliefs can vary widely.

9. Mormonism – Jesus, spirit brother of Satan, was once a man like all men; one of their doctrines is God was once a man like us; salvation by faith in their Jesus, being obedient to Mormonism and good works; non-Mormons get a second chance after death to convert; best Mormons get their own universe and become its god; worst of the worst are cast into eternal darkness; claims to be the only true church. Also known by Church of Jesus Christ of Latter Day Saints or LDS.

10. Jehovah's Witnesses – Jesus is not God. Jesus is the archangel Michael; salvation by faith in Jesus plus works and obedience to JW teaching; most believers live eternally on a renewed Earth since they believe heaven is full; non-believers die, cease to exist; claims to be the only true church.

11. Atheism/Humanism – Jesus just a man; no afterlife; die, buried.

Our list indicates that New Age believers, Mormons, Jehovah's Witnesses and others believe Jesus existed, but their versions of Jesus contradict the Bible and each other. Muslims say that Jesus existed, but he did not die on the cross and rise again. Most religions say that Jesus was just a man.

The Bible reveals that Jesus is God in the flesh and the only way to heaven. Not everyone can be correct. To come to a version of Jesus which is contrary to the Bible, people often arbitrarily reject parts of the Bible they do not like and build their own Jesus. Then they add other books with teachings that contradict what Jesus taught, and with no evidence, they claim that these are correct, and the Bible is false. Although this list is not all-inclusive, the contradictions are even more abundant when you add others.

If the evidence shows us that God does exist, we will be utilizing the law of non- contradiction to eliminate those beliefs that contradict the truth. I want to reiterate that we should respect others and co-exist with them. Every person has the right to believe whatever they want, and no one has the right to force their beliefs on anyone. But the truth of the matter is simply stated in the following quote:

—Contrary beliefs can exist but contrary truths cannot.‖ Dr. Frank Turek, author, I Don't Have Enough Faith to Be an Atheist.

Narrow-Minded and Intolerant Christians

Christianity is often considered intolerant and is frequently rejected for pointing out that Jesus claimed to be the only way to heaven.

Jesus said to him, "I am the way, and the truth, and the life. No one comes to the Father except through me. John 14:6

But as you can see from the list, when it comes to salvation and eternity, most beliefs are exclusive. Atheism, for example, is very exclusive and if it is true, none of the other beliefs can be true. The truth here is that the followers of each belief claim they have found the truth. No one would place their faith in something they knew for certain was a lie.

The exceptions would be beliefs like New Age and a Higher Power that embrace contradictions. These teachings to some degree are saying that all or many beliefs are equally true. Therefore, truth can contradict itself, which we know is impossible, since we understand how truth works.

Therefore, the question remains: who has the truth?

Action Taken Upon Established Truth

My favorite definition for the Christian faith is action taken upon established truth. Think about this for a moment. It says that something actually happened in history that made the first believers take action by placing their faith in Jesus as their Savior. The disciples testified that Jesus proved to be trustworthy, and He backed up His bold claims right before their eyes. They concluded, based on Jesus' miracles and the resurrection, that it was reasonable to trust Him regarding all that He said eternity holds.

Some people claim that you do not need evidence for a belief in God. But based on what we see in the Bible, Jesus clearly disagrees. Trusting in feelings alone or in what others believe is why so many people are led astray. The Christian faith is not an exercise in imagination, nor is it founded on feelings. It is based on real historical events seen and reported by eyewitnesses. Additionally, we have Old Testament prophecies that reveal the coming Messiah. When Jesus showed up claiming to be God, the facts say He fulfilled those prophecies, performed miracles and rose from the dead to prove His identity.

He (Jesus) presented himself alive to them after his suffering by many proofs, appearing to them during forty days and speaking about the kingdom of God (Acts 1:3, emphasis added).

"But if I do them, even though you do not believe me, believe the works (miracles), that you may know and understand that the Father is in me and I am in the Father" (John 10:38, emphasis added).

According to the Bible, the apostle Paul (an eyewitness to the resurrected Jesus -1 Cor 15:8) went to the Jewish temples and reasoned with the Jews that Jesus was the Messiah. In this next verse, Paul clearly tells us that a Christian's faith is in vain if the resurrection did not actually occur:

And if Christ has not been raised, then our preaching is in vain and your faith is in vain (1 Cor. 15:14).

I agree with Paul, and I would not be a Christian if the facts we can investigate indicated that something else was true. If any belief about God is false, including Christianity, then all the faith in the world will not make it true.

You may claim that miracles are not possible, and that life cannot come from non-life, thus making resurrection impossible, and a Christian's faith in vain. If God does not exist, I agree. But if the facts say God does exist, you cannot rule out miracles, including the resurrection. Therefore, our next step is to examine the scientific facts to see if God exists. Later we will examine the facts to see if it is reasonable to trust the Bible's claims.

Conclusion – The Christian faith is founded on historical events like the resurrection, which can be investigated. The disciples placed their faith in Jesus because He proved His claim to be God to them.

Best Fits the Evidence

While we cannot prove God's existence and identity empirically (repeated testing and observation) as we can with gravity, many believe the evidence proves it is true beyond a reasonable doubt. This is the same standard that is used every day in our court system.

Jim Wallace is a cold case homicide detective who converted from atheism to Christianity based on the evidence. He states on his website http://coldcasechristianity.com/ that when he pulls a case file off the shelf, his job is to find the suspect who best fits the evidence. Imagine that you are a detective and there are twenty pieces of evidence and five suspects. If five details fit one suspect, it's not a big deal. But you would get excited if the same suspect popped up time and again as a match to the facts. Now if one suspect matched twenty out of twenty pieces of evidence, Jim would tell us this suspect is the guilty party or the most unlucky person in the world. He uses the same logic to find the truth about God's existence and identity, and so must we. So, let's pull God's Cold Case file off your shelf, dust it off and see what best fits the evidence.

Motivation for Your Investigation

Approximately 155,000 people die around the world every day. Virtually none of us are certain of when our day will come. What is on the other side of death? Do we rot in the ground, or do we have another destination? The Bible offers only two options—heaven or hell—and it reveals these truths:

1. If it is true, like all truth, it applies to you whether you believe it or not.

2. If you reject God, you will be without excuse, even if you have never read the Bible.

The Bible guarantees that God is so obvious through creation and in our conscience that those who deny Him are without excuse. Consider the following verses:

They show that the work of the law is written on their hearts, while their conscience also bears witness, and their conflicting thoughts accuse or even excuse them (Rom. 2:15, emphasis added).

For his invisible attributes, namely, his eternal power and divine nature, have been clearly perceived, ever since the creation of the world, in the things that have been made. So they are without excuse (Rom. 1:20, emphasis added).

So, before you scoff and say that God or hell do not exist, as some do, let's keep the claims of these two verses in mind, examine the facts, read the supporting quotes from experts in the field and weigh the evidence. Consider the following testimony of Detective Jim Wallace:

—I was an atheist for 35 years. I was passionate in my opposition to Christianity, and I enjoyed debating my Christian friends. I seldom found them prepared to defend what they believed. I became a police officer and eventually advanced to detective. Along the way, I developed a healthy respect for the role of evidence in discerning truth, and my profession gave me ample opportunity to press into practice what I learned about the nature and power of evidence. Throughout all of this, I remained an angry atheist, hostile to Christianity and largely dismissive of Christians. But if I am honest with you, I'll have to admit that I never took the time to examine the evidence for the Christian Worldview without the bias and presupposition of naturalism. I never gave the case for Christianity a fair shake.When I finally examined the evidence fairly, I found it difficult to deny, especially if I hoped to retain my respect for the way evidence is utilized to determine truth. I found the evidence for Christianity to be convincing.‖ Jim Wallace, http://coldcasechristianity.com/

Does God Exist?

The Universe Had a Beginning

The basic cosmological argument for the beginning of the universe states:

1. Everything that comes into existence requires a cause.

2. The universe came into existence out of nothing.

3. Therefore, the universe requires a cause.

Logic and reason tell us that something that does not exist cannot bring itself into existence. For example: before you were born, could you have brought yourself into existence, or would a cause outside yourself (your parents) be required? If there was not a cause outside yourself, you would not exist now. The universe is larger, but the same obvious truth applies.

—To continue to look for a natural cause for the beginning of the universe, when natural laws did not yet exist, is like spending your life trying to prove you gave birth to your mother.‖ Dr. Frank Turek, author and speaker, I Don't Have Enough Faith to Be an Atheist.

Science is the search for causes, and every effect has a cause. Here are a couple of the numerous facts that indicate the universe had a beginning:

1. Einstein's Theory of Relativity demands a beginning to time, space and matter and says they are co-relative, meaning one cannot exist without the other.

2. The undisputed Second Law of Thermodynamics tells us the universe is running out of usable energy and heading from order to chaos. Scientists tell us if the universe had always existed, we would be out of usable energy and in complete chaos by now.

The scientific evidence clearly shows that our entire universe (time, space, matter, energy), including all natural laws, leapt into being out of nothing. The cause of the universe must be outside of and separate from the universe itself, which is a definition of supernatural. It must be incredibly powerful, because it created everything out of nothing. It must be eternal, because it created time. It must be immaterial, because it created material. These facts fit the the God of the Bible, a theistic God, a God who created and sustains the universe but is separate from creation.

Consider this simple analogy I learned from Ray Comfort at livingwaters.com. When you look at a building, how do you know there was a builder? You have never seen or met him. Isn't the building itself absolute proof there was a builder? When you look at a painting, how do you know there was a painter? Isn't the painting itself absolute proof there was a painter? So, when you learn that the entire universe was created out of nothing before natural laws existed, how do you know there is a creator? You have never seen or met Him. Like the building and the painting, isn't the universe itself absolute proof of a creator?

"The universe had a beginning. There was once nothing and now there is something." Janna Levin, Department of Applied Mathematics and Theoretical Physics at Cambridge University (emphasis added).

"The conclusion of this lecture is that the universe has not existed forever. Rather, the universe, and time itself, had a beginning in the Big Bang." Stephen Hawking, Theoretical physicist, Beginning of Time (emphasis added).

"The scientific evidence is now overwhelming that the universe began with a 'Bang'. The Big Bang theory is the most widely accepted theory of the creation of the universe." Dr. Vander Pluijm University of Michigan, www.godandscience.org (emphasis added)

Robert Jastrow, an agnostic astronomer who sat at the Hubble telescope, stated the following in an interview. —Astronomers now find they have painted themselves into a corner because they have proven, by their own methods, that the world began abruptly in an act of creation to which you can trace the seeds of every star, every planet, every living thing in this cosmos and on the Earth. And they have found that all this happened as a product of forces you cannot hope to discover... that there are what I or anyone would call supernatural forces at work is now, I think, a scientifically proven fact.‖ —A Scientist Caught Between Two Faiths‖ Christianity Today, August 6, 1982 (emphasis added).

—A universe that came from nothing in the big bang will disappear into nothing at the big crunch, its glorious few zillion years of existence not even a memory.‖ British astrophysicist Paul Davies, www.thinkexist.com (emphasis added)

Conclusion – The universe (time, space, matter and energy) had a beginning. By necessity, there must be an eternal, uncaused first cause for anything to exist now. God is the most logical explanation.

Who Made God?

Many people think they have come up with a great objection when they ask the question who made God? The answer is simple—no one. Only things that begin to exist require a cause. That's why people have such a hard time figuring out the mind-numbing problem of which came first—the chicken or the egg? We know if one did not exist before the other, neither would exist now. Since the universe is not eternal, by necessity there must be an initial uncaused eternal cause outside of the natural universe, or nothing would exist now.

The eternal God is your dwelling place (Deut. 33:27, emphasis added).

The Universe and Life Are Designed - The Teleological (design) argument for God

1. All design requires a designer.

2. The universe and life exhibit intricate design.

3. Therefore, the universe and life require a designer.

There are only two types of causes: natural and intelligent. Common sense tells us the Grand Canyon had a natural cause and Mount Rushmore had an intelligent cause. We have a natural ability to spot intelligent design even in the simplest form, like a footprint in the sand or a heart carved in a tree. The SETI (Search for Extraterrestrial Intelligence) program would be thrilled to hear even a very simple organized message from outer space on one of their radio telescopes. They would immediately know that it indicated intelligent life. Yet decades of listening have produced no solid evidence. So, if a simple message from outer space or the words on this page require intelligence, what about the most intricate design known to man?

Our planet is designed specifically for life. Astrophysicist Hugh Ross maintains a growing list of 122 constants—Anthropic Principles that are set on a razor's edge. Alter any one just slightly, and in most cases, we would not exist. I have listed six for you to consider:

1. If the universe expanded at a rate one millionth more slowly than it does, the universe would not exist.

2. If Jupiter was not in its current orbit, its gravitational force could not protect us from comets that could destroy the Earth.

3. Earth's rotation: if longer, temperature differences would be too great; if shorter, atmospheric wind velocities would be too great

4. If the Earth's 23-degree axle tilt was altered even slightly, temperatures would be too extreme for life.

5. Oxygen to nitrogen ratio in the atmosphere: if larger, life functions would proceed too quickly; if smaller, life functions would proceed too slowly.

6. Magnetic field: if stronger, electromagnetic storms would be too severe; if weaker, no protection from solar wind particles.

Dr. Ross has calculated —the odds of these 122 constants that make it possible for our existence, being precisely as they are at one chance in 10^{138}. In mathematics this means: one chance in one with 138 zeros after it.‖ Dr. Hugh Ross, Why I believe in Divine Creation, www.reasons.org

To help put this number into perspective: statistical zero, where scientists usually write something off as impossible, is one in 10^{50}: one with 50 zeros after it. NOAA places the odds of being hit by lightning at one in a million, or one with six zeros after it. Your odds of winning the California Super Lotto are one chance in 41,416,353 or a 4 followed by seven zeros (approximately).

John O'Keefe (astronomer at NASA): "We are, by astronomical standards, a pampered, cosseted, cherished group of creatures. If the Universe had not been made with the most exacting precision we could never have come into existence. It is my view that these circumstances indicate the universe was created for man to live in." Heeren, F. 1995. Show Me God. Wheeling, IL, Searchlight Publications, p. 200 (emphasis added).

"The laws [of physics] seem to be the product of exceedingly ingenious design. The universe must have a purpose.‖ Paul Davies: British astrophysicist, Davies, P. 1984, Superforce: The Search for a Grand Unified Theory of Nature (emphasis added).

"Astronomy leads us to a unique event, a universe which was created out of nothing, one with the very delicate balance needed to provide exactly the conditions required to permit life, and one which has an underlying (one might say 'supernatural') plan." Arno Penzias, Nobel Prize in physics, quoted in Cosmos, Bios, Theos: Scientists Reflect on Science, God, and the Origins of the Universe, Life, and Homo Sapiens (emphasis added).

"The exquisite order displayed by our scientific understanding of the physical world calls for the divine." Vera Kistiakowsky, MIT physicist, quoted in Cosmos, Bios, Theos: Scientists Reflect on Science, God, and the Origins of the Universe, Life, and Homo Sapiens (emphasis added).

—Is it possible that design happens by chance without a designer? There is perhaps one chance in a trillion that _S.O.S.‘ could be written in the sand by the wind. But who would use a one-in-a-trillion explanation? Someone once said that if you sat a million monkeys at a million typewriters for a million years, one of them would eventually type out all of Hamlet by chance. But when we find the text of Hamlet, we don't wonder whether it came from chance and monkeys. Why then does the atheist use that incredibly improbable explanation for the universe? Clearly, because it is his only chance of remaining an atheist. At this point we need a psychological explanation of the atheist rather than a logical explanation of the universe. We have a logical explanation of the universe, but the atheist does not like it. It's called God.‖ Peter Kreeft, Ph.D., Professor of philosophy at Boston College, www.peterkreeft.com

Conclusion – Intricate design in the universe requires an intelligent designer.

Complex Design of Life

One of many things naturalists cannot explain is the source of information. How could non-living chemicals have come together by accident to produce the highly complex information found in DNA? We know that all information, written languages or codes always come from an information-rich source—a mind. Minds create intelligent communication, not natural causes. Life's design displays a level of complexity far beyond anything we know of.

—(1) DNA is not merely a molecule with a pattern; it is a code, a language, and an information storage mechanism. (2) All codes we know the origin of are created by a conscious mind. (3) Therefore DNA was designed by a mind, and language and information are proof of the action of a Super intelligence.‖ Perry Marshall, Information Specialist, www.cosmicfingerprints.com

—All instruction, all teaching, all training comes with intent. Someone who writes an instruction manual does so with purpose. Did you know that in every cell of our bodies there exists a very detailed instruction code, much like a miniature computer program? A computer program is made up of ones and zeros, like this: 110010101011000. The ways they are arranged tell the computer program what to do. The DNA code in each of our cells is very similar. It's made up of four chemicals that scientists abbreviate as A, T, G, and C. These are arranged in the human cell like this: CGTGTGACTCGCTCCTGAT and so on. There are three billion of these letters in every human cell! Well, just like you can program your phone to beep for specific reasons, DNA instructs the cell. DNA is a three- billion-lettered program telling the cell to act in a certain way. It is a full instruction manual. Natural, biological causes are completely lacking as an explanation when programmed information is involved. You cannot find instruction, precise information like this, without someone intentionally constructing it.‖ Francis S. Collins, director of the Human Genome Project, and author of The Language of God, Free Press, New York, NY, 2006, www.everystudent.com (emphasis added).

—The amount of information that could be contained in a pinhead volume of DNA, if all the information were written into paperback books, would make a pile of such books 500 times higher than from here to the moon! Dr. Werner Gitt Creationist Information Scientist, www.creation.com

—The human eye is a truly amazing phenomenon. Although accounting for just one fourth-thousandth of an adult's weight, it is the medium which processes some 80% of the information received by its owner from the outside world. The tiny retina contains about 130 million rod-shaped cells, which detect light intensity and transmit impulses to the visual cortex of the brain by means of some one million nerve fibers, while nearly six million cone-shaped cells do the same job, but respond specifically to color variation. The eyes can handle 500,000 messages simultaneously, and are kept clear by ducts producing just the right amount of fluid with which the lids clean both eyes simultaneously in one five- thousandth of a second. John Blanchard, Does God Believe in Atheists? 2000, p. 213.

—Human DNA is like a computer program but far, far more advanced than any software ever created. Microsoft's Bill Gates, The Road Ahead (emphasis added).

"Although I was once sharply critical of the argument to design, I have since come to see that, when correctly formatted, this argument constitutes a persuasive case for the existence of God. Anthony Flew, atheist for 50 years, There is a God, p. 95 (emphasis added).

Conclusion – Intricate design in life requires an intelligent designer.

Could the Universe or Life be an Accident?

—The calculations of Oxford mathematician Roger Penrose show the improbability of a universe conducive to life occurring by accident, luck and chance is one chance in $10^{10^{123}}$. The phrase _extremely unlikely' is inadequate to describe this possibility. It is hard even to imagine what this number means. In math, the value 10^{123} means 1 followed by 123 zeros. This is more than the total number of atoms (10^{78}, one with 78 zeros) believed to exist in the entire universe. But Penrose's answer is vastly more than this: It requires one followed by 10^{123} zeros. It is impossible.‖ Roger Penrose, The Emperor's New Mind; from Michael Denton's Nature's Destiny.

—As biochemists discover more and more about the awesome complexity of life, it is apparent that its chances of originating by accident are so minute that they can be completely ruled out. Life cannot have arisen by chance.‖ Sir Fred Hoyle, Intelligent Universe.

—An honest man, armed with all the knowledge available to us now, could only state that in some sense, the origin of life appears at the moment to be almost a miracle, so many are the conditions which would have had to have been satisfied to get it going.‖ Francis Crick, molecular biologist, biophysicist, and neuroscientist, co-discoverer of the structure of the DNA molecule, Life Itself, Simon and Schuster.

—In the last thirty years a number of prominent scientists have attempted to calculate the odds that a free-living, single-celled organism, such as a bacterium, might result by the chance combining of pre-existent building blocks. Harold Morowitz calculated the odds as one chance in $10^{100,000,000,000}$ (one chance in one with 100 trillion zeros after it). Sir Fred Hoyle calculated the odds of only the proteins of an amoebae arising by chance as one chance in $10^{40,000}$. The odds calculated by

Morowitz and Hoyle are staggering. Mathematicians tell us that any event with an improbability greater than one chance in 1050 is in the realm of metaphysics --i.e. a miracle.‖ Mark Eastman, MD, Creation by Design, T.W.F.T. Publishers, 1996, 21-22, www.allaboutthejourney.org

—It is a shock to us in the twentieth century to discover, from observations science has made, that the fundamental mechanisms of life cannot be ascribed to natural selection, and therefore were designed. But we must deal with our shock as best we can and go on.‖ Michael Behe, Ph.D. Professor Biochemistry, Molecular Machines, Cosmic Pursuit, Spring 1998, p. 35.

Making Frankenstein

In the unlikely event scientists are able to create even the simplest life from non- living chemicals, would this accomplishment rule out the need for an Intelligent Creator? No, it would instead support the case for a Creator, because it demonstrates that it takes centuries of man's intelligence to create life, rather than accident, luck, chance and time as naturalism states. You must remember that the facts tell us everything came from nothing. In trying to create life, scientists do not start with nothing, because we cannot even create a grain of sand out of nothing.

Conclusion – The facts prove that the probability of the universe and life happening by accident, luck and chance are beyond impossible. Both require an intelligent cause.

Why this is Not the God of the Gaps

Skeptics accuse those who believe in God of just inserting God as the answer when the cause is unknown. This has been true at times in the past (—Thunder! The gods must be mad!‖), and it may be true today for some primitive tribes. But scientists who support Intelligent Design follow the evidence where it leads. If there is a natural explanation, that's fine, but when 100 percent of the observable evidence says a natural explanation is impossible, then intelligence is considered.

Here are some perfect examples: if something can pop into existence out of nothing, uncaused, then why would it only happen to the universe? Why not all kinds of things? Has it ever been observed? No—so the universe cannot be an exception. When it comes to design, have you ever seen a complex message, code, information or written instructions come from anything but a mind? Have scientists? No, so the complex message in DNA requires a mind as its source. It could not happen by accident. Has life ever been observed to come from non-life by accident, luck, chance and time? No, none of the items I have just listed have been observed. There is no proof that these things can happen by accident, luck, chance and time. If they did happen on their own, but do not happen on a regular basis, by definition they would be a miracle. Therefore, to be an atheist and believe the universe, life, information and complex design came about by accident, the person must exercise faith in miracles without a miracle worker.

"It's not just that we lack a natural explanation for the genetic code, but that such a message is positive, empirically verifiable evidence for an intelligent being. So we are not going on what we don't know, but what we do know." Dr. Frank Turek, Crossexamined.org, email message.

Evolution

Evolution happens, but the facts do not support macroevolution (the theory that one species evolved from another). Microevolution is visible when a bacterium transforms to develop a resistance to an antibiotic, but it's still bacteria. It is also visible in different breeds of dogs—but they are still dogs. There has never been solid evidence for macroevolution. If it were true, scientists would not still be looking for the first fossil record of a missing link; they would have found millions of them by now. Supposed amazing discoveries of the missing link with the Nebraska Man, Lucy, Piltdown Man, Ramapithecus, Java Man, Peking Man and others have all been debunked as fakes.

—The chance that higher life forms might have emerged (through evolutionary processes) is comparable with the chance that a 'tornado sweeping through a junk yard might assemble a Boeing 747 from the material therein.' Sir Fred Hoyle, professor of astronomy, —Hoyle on Evolution, Nature, Vol. 294, November 12, 1981, p. 105.

—None exists in the literature claiming that one species has been shown to evolve into another. Bacteria, the simplest form of independent life, are ideal for this kind of study, with generation times of twenty to thirty minutes, and populations achieved after eighteen hours. But throughout 150 years of the science of bacteriology, there is no evidence that one species of bacteria has changed into another. British bacteriologist Alan H. Linton, —Scant Search for the Maker, The Times Higher Education Supplement, April 20, 2001 (emphasis added).

Currently, more than 600 scientists have signed the following statement, with the number continuing to grow. –We are skeptical of claims for the ability of random mutation and natural selection to account for the complexity of life. Careful examination of the evidence for Darwinian theory should be encouraged. www.dissentfromdarwin.org

Read a more detailed version of this book, including more answers about evolution: God-Evidence-Truth.com.

Why Can't Some Scientists See God in the Facts?

That's a very important question, and much of it has to do with the definition of science. The following primary definition of science in

the American Heritage Dictionary,
http://education.yahoo.com/reference/dictionary/entry/science ,
restricts the search to a natural cause:

a) The observation, identification, description, experimental investigation, and theoretical explanation of phenomena.

b) Such activities restricted to a class of natural phenomena.

c) Such activities applied to an object of inquiry or study.

By definition, science rules out God before looking at the evidence. The restriction to natural causes requires scientists to at times try to force a square peg into a round hole, suggesting things happened by accident, luck, chance and time that have never been observed.

—We take the side of science in spite of the patent absurdity of some of its constructs, in spite of its failure to fulfill many of its extravagant promises of health and life, and in spite of the tolerance of the scientific community for unsubstantiated just-so-stories, because we have a prior commitment, a commitment to materialism. It is not that the methods and institutions of science somehow compel us to accept a material explanation of the phenomenal world, but, on the contrary, that we are forced by our priori adherence to material causes to create an apparatus of investigation and a set of concepts that produce material explanations, no matter how counterintuitive, no matter how mystifying to the uninitiated. Moreover, that materialism is an absolute, for we cannot allow a Divine Foot in the door." Professor Richard Lewontin, a geneticist and evolutionist, Billions and Billions of Demons (emphasis added).

—Ultimately it is all about the concept of _God.' No answer can be "God probably did it" for a scientist, by definition, because God is defined as being non- materialistic or outside of Nature. Therefore, scientists commonly argue that God, if he even exists, is beyond the detection of science—that he cannot be ruled in or out of any equation.‖ Sean Pitman M.D. www.DetectingDesign.com (emphasis added).

You will seek me and find me, when you seek me with all your heart (Jeremiah 29:13).

The atheist and many scientists can't find God for the same reason that a thief can't find a policeman.

Aliens Brought us Here

Even though people have claimed to have seen UFOs, there's no solid evidence from any of the SETI programs, which began in the early 1960s. Some widely speculative scientists, even the champion of today's atheism, Oxford Professor Richard Dawkins, suggest (with no credible evidence) that aliens could be the cause of life on Earth. Hollywood has helped foster this theory in our imagination with their realistic science fiction movies. But even if aliens exist, this does not address the fact that the universe leapt into being out of nothing, and only pushes back the creation of life one step; who created the aliens? By necessity, there must be an uncaused first cause.

Could the real origin for this display of blind faith by some scientists come from their knowledge that it is impossible for non-living chemicals to come together by accident and form life? Rejecting God before they even look at the evidence, they now find themselves boxed in a corner with only aliens as a way to introduce intelligence. Aliens may exist, but they're not the best fit to the evidence.

Do any Scientists Believe in God?

Yes, according to surveys, roughly 51% of scientists believe in God in some form:
http://www.pewforum.org/2009/11/05/scientists-and-belief/.

There are people with great human intelligence on both sides of the debate about God. Since both sides cannot be right, we see man's worldly intelligence may not always be the indicator of truth.

—Science without religion is lame, religion without science is blind.‖ Albert Einstein, German-born US physicist, —Science, Philosophy and Religion: a Symposium." 1941.

The Moral Argument for God's Existence

It's a universal fact that everyone (including atheists) has a conscience which deals exclusively with morality and to which we feel a sense of obligation. A sane person would never consider living in total rebellion to their conscience. No one needs the Bible to know right from wrong. Our conscience acts as a warning system in an attempt to stop us from making the wrong decision by illuminating what we ought and ought not to do. The question is, how could everyone in the world have essentially the same warning system which informs them it is wrong to lie, steal and murder, unless God exists? Some argue this comes from evolution, our parents and society. I agree that morality is passed down and reinforced by them, but the question is not how we learn it, but why our conscience recognizes that some acts—like murder and rape—are unquestionably wrong.

If we were to examine the life of the one person who appeared to possess the highest level of morality among humans, we all know they would not be perfect. They would simply be closer to perfection than you or I. But what are we comparing that nearly perfect person with, to realize they fall short? We must be utilizing a higher standard that we are all aware exists. Why would we have a sense of what perfect morality is if it does not exist in humans? Many believe the best explanation is that God exists and He placed morality within us, as the Bible claims.

They (mankind) show that the work of the law is written on their hearts, while their conscience also bears witness, and their conflicting thoughts accuse or even excuse them (Rom. 2:15, emphasis added).

Actions vs. Reactions in Moral Issues

This is important to understand and keep in mind as you read this section: we recognize objective morality better by our reactions than by our actions. For example: If I steal twenty dollars from you, I may not think it is wrong. But as soon as you steal twenty dollars from me, I know for certain it is wrong.

We all know that it's wrong to lie and steal, and if we get caught, we make excuses. Why make excuses if it's not wrong? When someone lies or steals from us, we immediately know it is wrong. A great way to realize if what you want to do is right or wrong is to consider how you would react if it were done to you.

And as you wish that others would do to you, do so to them (Luke 6:31).

Objective versus Individual Opinion

Some claim that morality is relative or subjective (one opinion versus another), therefore making God unnecessary. On the other hand, objective morality, values and duties indicate a moral truth that rises above all people, a moral truth that still would be true even if everyone were brainwashed to believe it was not. If our conscience—our knowledge of right and wrong—is more than just our opinion, it must have a source that transcends (is above and beyond) humanity. Therefore, if it is, in fact, true that objective morality does exist, its logical source is a moral law giver. In other words, God.

Dr. William Lane Craig of reasonablefaith.org lays out the Moral Argument for God's existence:

1. If God does not exist, objective moral values and duties do not exist.

2. Objective moral values and duties do exist.

3. Therefore, God exists.

Next, we will be examining the evidence to see if the second point is true. Is morality objective, or just opinion? If the second point is true, this logical argument for God's existence is sound.

Objective Morality Test

The following test will help you see that objective morality does exist and therefore God exists. It uses real-life graphic examples of situations which some claim are acceptable. This leads to the assertion by others that morality is just one opinion versus another. As you read, mentally place yourself in the victim's position and decide if the actions are wrong despite the opinions of the perpetrators.

1. You are one of the abused children.

In an 8-3-11 AFP article on the internet entitled —US Charges 72 Over 'Nightmare' Child Porn Network,‖ horrific sexual acts done to young children are described.

The accused believe that what they were doing was proper conduct and not illegal or immoral. They were essentially torturing young children for their fun and pleasure. Consider this quote:

"Dreamboard's creators and members lived all over the world—but they allegedly were united by a disturbing belief that the sexual abuse of children is proper conduct that should not be criminalized.ǁ Attorney Eric Holder.

2. You are one of those tortured and murdered.

When the Nazis were arrested and put on trial for crimes against humanity, their defense was the claim that outsiders had no right to come in and tell them how they should run their society. They were just following orders, and they claimed that torturing and murdering millions of innocent people was not wrong.

3. You are the designated non-person.

We see something unique when we compare abortion, slavery and the Nazis' killing of the Jews. For years, America condoned slavery by designating slaves as non-persons or property. The Nazis in their day and radical Muslims today consider Jews non-persons. Ironically, unborn children in the United States are considered non-persons too. If they were designated persons, they would automatically have rights under our constitution to life, liberty and the pursuit of happiness. If the unborn were considered persons, abortion would automatically be illegal in the United States.

So, if some classified you a non-person— making it legal to take your life—would it still be wrong?

If you followed my instructions and mentally placed yourself in the victim's role, you know absolutely that these actions are wrong, even though some claim they are okay. For a person to maintain a belief that morality is just personal opinion, they would need to say all three examples are perfectly acceptable.

In addition, elaborate attempts to get around our knowledge of what we know is wrong, along with attempts to cover it up, make it obvious that moral law is objective. If morality was just one opinion versus another, 9/11 was not wrong. No one should be punished and everyone needs to be let out of jail. No one could take a moral stand against anything and there would be no need to define Jews, slaves and the unborn as non-persons in an attempt to cover up immoral actions.

I believe our test conclusively proves that objective morality exists. Therefore, the second point of Dr. Craig's moral argument is true; which makes the conclusion of the argument true. The moral law we all know exists, points to a law giver. Logically God exists.

Moral Conflicts

Alleged moral conflicts have a reasonable explanation if you investigate. Humans have selfish desires and tend to ignore truths that do not fit into their agenda. The Bible says we suppress the truth by denying or creating our own god to do the things we want.

For the wrath of God is revealed from heaven against all ungodliness and unrighteousness of men, who by their unrighteousness suppress the truth (Rom. 1:18, emphasis added).

Some say abortion is acceptable and some say it is not, which leads some to claim that morality is just opinion. But this disagreement is really about when life begins. The pro-life side says life begins at conception, while the pro-choice side says it begins at birth. Therefore abortion is not taking a life to someone pro-choice. Yet even those who say abortion is justifiable will passionately defend a newborn baby. Both sides agree life is valuable, but they disagree on when it begins. However, I would bet that anyone who is pro-choice would quickly change their mind if they were still in the womb and their mother walked into an abortion clinic.

—Some might argue: Aren't there moral conflicts as well? Some cultures permit polygamy, for instance. Yes, but marriage customs and vows that bind marriages together also prohibit adultery. While applications and expressions of moral principles may differ from culture to culture, there are basic moral principles that cut across cultural lines.‖ Paul Copan, www.4truth.net, www.paulcopan.com

Moral Obligations are Only to Persons

Some people claim that God is an impersonal force. One of the problems with this theory is that we never feel moral obligations to impersonal forces like gravity, only to other persons. The sense of moral obligation we experience supports the existence of a personal, theistic God as described in the Bible.

Right and Wrong, Just and Unjust

To bring the undeniable knowledge of right and wrong to the forefront of your mind, please read the following list and sincerely consider the injustice in our world. If you have experienced injustice in your own life, bring that to mind also.

Many innocent people died on 9/11. Millions of innocent people have died in wars. Some kill others, claiming God's approval. Innocent children are kidnapped and killed. Others are randomly murdered. Adults sexually abuse innocent children. Over 30,000 children die every day of hunger and preventable diseases, 24 every minute. Wrongfully accused people are in prison right now. Simply professing to trust Jesus in strict Muslim countries can lead to imprisonment, torture and death. Some are wealthy beyond belief simply because of their family. Some are rich from crime. Many work hard and are still poor.

If the items listed stir your conscience, it is because you know they are unfair and unjust. The question is, does this profound sense of injustice that you experience when you review these facts have any meaning, or is this inner sense simply a worthless illusion?

Philosopher Immanuel Kant, in the following moral argument for God's existence, concluded that if this inborn sense of right and wrong, just and unjust has any meaning at all, the following must exist:

1. There must be justice. Since there is not justice in this life, there must be life after death.

2. For justice, there must be a judgment.

3. For perfect judgment, a perfect moral judge must exist.

4. The judge must have all knowledge, so he cannot make an error in judgment.

5. The judge must be all-powerful, so he can carry out any punishment he imposes on the guilty.

Kant's conclusion points to the God of the Bible without using the Bible and further confirms the necessity of God's existence.

—Everyone knows certain principles; there is no land where murder is a virtue and gratitude a vice.ll U of T Professor and author J. Budziszewski, Written on the Heart: The Case for Natural Law.

—In moral experience we apprehend a realm of moral values and duties that impose themselves upon us. There's no more reason to deny the objective reality of moral values than the objective reality of the physical world.ll William Lane Craig, www.reasonablefaith.org

Moral Evil Proves There is no God

I agree, if I only focused on the evil in the world, I would have a hard time believing God exists. But evil does not disprove the existence of God, especially in the light of all of the evidence that indicates God is a necessity. Man's ability to commit evil is due to our free will, the source of all moral evil. God knew evil would exist with free will, and He knew man would crucify His only Son, but He still gave us free will. To stop evil, God would need to remove everyone's free will, which would remove our ability to love. God obviously places a very high value on love. Can you imagine a world where love was not possible? The Bible promises that God will stop evil, but in His time, not ours.

I also want to point out that our ability to recognize evil supports the existence of God. To judge something as evil requires the knowledge of what is good. To judge something imperfect requires the knowledge of what is perfect. C.S Lewis explains:

—As an atheist my argument against God was that the universe seemed so cruel and unjust. But how had I got this idea of just and unjust? A man does not call a line crooked unless he has some idea of a straight line. What was I comparing this universe with when I called it unjust?‖ C.S. Lewis, Mere Christianity.

Religion has a Terrible Record of Immorality

It is true that some have used Christianity as an excuse to do evil, and it is wrong. However, all the injustices done in the last 2,000 years by people who claim to be Christians do not prove the Bible is false, any more than a bad cop proves the entire police force and its mission corrupt.

Those who put forth this objection demonstrate their lack of understanding of Jesus's teachings. This objection is utterly defeated simply by understanding what Jesus taught, which helps us identify a follower of Christ. The two main principles Jesus taught that apply here are to love your enemies and that there will be false believers who will cause problems.

"You have heard that it was said, „You shall love your neighbor and hate your enemy." But I say to you, Love your enemies and pray for those who persecute you" (Matthew 5:43-44).

In reference to those who put Him on the cross: *Jesus said, "Father, forgive them, for they know not what they do" (Luke 23:34a).*

In the Bible, a sinner is at enmity (an enemy) with God, yet the sinner is exactly who Jesus died to save.

...but God shows his love for us in that while we were still sinners, Christ died for us (Romans 5:8).

Bible provides a very clear warning of false prophets, teachers, and imposters. It tells us that God is aware of this, and they may fool us, but they're not fooling God.

Jesus had twelve main disciples. One of them was Judas Iscariot, who would have appeared to everyone to be a follower of Christ. Yet he betrayed Jesus and set him up to be arrested and crucified. Do you think Judas Iscariot was a Christian or a false believer?

Then Judas Iscariot, who was one of the twelve, went to the chief priests in order to betray him to them (Mark 14:10).

"Not everyone who calls out to me, 'Lord! Lord!' will enter the Kingdom of Heaven. Only those who actually do the will of my Father in heaven will enter" (Matthew 7:21)

Yet because of false brothers secretly brought in (Galatians 2:4a).

Just go into a Christian church today and see what they are teaching. No true believer is preaching a sermon on how to kill non-believers who refuse to convert to Christianity. A belief in Jesus must be made freely.

—Religion does not poison man, man poisons religion.‖ Dr. Frank Turek, www.crossexamined.org

—Let's be honest. There are guys today who bomb abortion clinics. There are people today who establish their own compound, name it after their daddy, and are killing in the name of Christ. But here is the fundamental point. When these people kill in the name of Jesus, they are doing so in absolute defiance of the teachings of Christ. A Muslim will always bring up the Old Testament, David and Solomon. I say, that's great, but they're not my leader -- Jesus is. Jesus is God. That's the central point of Christianity. If Jesus isn't God, I'm wasting my time. Back to my point—these people do these violent things in defiance of Jesus' teaching. 'Pray for those who persecute you.' When a Muslim does these things in the name of Allah, he is doing so in strict adherence and allegiance to the teachings and example of Muhammad.‖ Dr. Ergun Caner, Muslim for half his life, Provost and Vice President of Academic Affairs, Arlington Baptist College.

—God is responsible for the fact of freedom. Humans are responsible for their acts of freedom.‖ http://www.youtube.com/watch?v=Rfd_1UAjelA

—The Crusades are often brought up as an excuse to reject Christianity by those who are not familiar with actual history. There were terrible things done in the Crusades, just as in any war. The intended purpose of the Crusades was not to force Christianity upon the unwilling, as some claim. History tells us the Crusades were a delayed response to Muslim aggression and their conquest of foreign lands.‖ Thomas Madden, —A Concise History of the Crusades.‖

The numbers killed by atheist regimes is staggering compared to all of those killed by Christianity. A full detailed version of this book, including those numbers, other questions and objections can be found online for free in an e-version at

Godevidencetruth.com. It can also be found by Googling: Gravity True For You But Not For Me.

Conclusion – Objective morality exists; it is displayed by one's conscience and is undeniable. It is similar to a law and all laws have lawgivers. A transcendent God is the best explanation.

The Facts Make Sense with God

If there is no God, what's the origin of information, intelligence, love, personality, feelings, common sense, the laws of logic, natural laws, knowledge, the laws of mathematics, emotions, the law of causality and all other immaterial things we know exist?

Those who claim there is no God believe everything has a natural or material explanation. The problem is that none of the items in the above list consist of material—yet they do exist. You would also need to explain the purpose of our existence. Most naturalists would say we have no purpose. But then the question is, why do the morally right thing? What obligates us to care for others if we are simply random chemicals that came together by accident, luck, chance and time? God's existence answers all of these questions and so many more.

Weighing the Facts, Does God Exist?

1. From the Cosmological Argument: 100 percent of the evidence tells us that everything that begins to exist requires a cause outside of itself. A cause outside of the universe would be supernatural, logically God. There is no evidence that things can come into existence uncaused. There must be an initial uncaused cause, something that has always existed, or nothing would exist now.

2. From the Design Argument: 100 percent of the evidence tells us any design, especially the highly complex design found in the

universe and life (DNA), requires a designer and only comes from a mind—God. Complex design, information and life have never been observed to come from non-life by accident, luck, chance and time.

3. From the Moral Argument: 100 percent of the evidence tells us that every law has a lawgiver and moral obligations are to persons, not impersonal forces. The conscience which crosses all languages, nations, genders and cultures is absolute proof of a transcendent lawgiver. God is a logical conclusion.

4. There is no evidence that life can come from non-life by accident, luck, chance and time. Abiogenesis has never been observed. Apart from a miracle, all the evidence indicates that life can only come from life: biogenesis. God's existence explains initial life.

Conclusion – God must exist!

No Excuse as Promised

An eternal, all-powerful God is an absolute necessity based on creation and our conscience. Science and our inherent knowledge of right and wrong validate the Bible's claim in Romans 1:20 that God is obvious and therefore man is without excuse. Can you imagine telling God you thought the intricate design of the universe came from nothing, without cause? That life came together by accident and you didn't realize it was wrong to violate your conscience?

Why We Cannot Rule Out Miracles

Since the solid evidence to this point indicates that by necessity, God must exist, you cannot rule out miracles. A miracle is an event that has no explanation in the natural and does not occur on a regular basis. Even atheists, who claim life came from non-life by accident, luck, chance and time in the beginning, must have faith that this miracle actually happened. There is no evidence to support their claim other than the fact that life exists, which does nothing to prove it. The truth is Christianity and atheism both require faith and miracles. Christians have a miracle worker and atheism claims miracles without a miracle worker. Christians have eyewitnesses to the resurrection who were willing to die for their testimony that life did come from non-life by the hand of God, when Jesus rose from the dead.

The biggest miracle in the Bible occurs in the first verse: In the beginning God created the heavens and the earth (Gen. 1:1). The universe and life were created out of nothing, as supported by the scientific evidence. If God can do that, then every miracle in the Bible is believable.

Since the evidence says God must exist, don't you think miracles—things that cannot happen in the natural and don't normally happen at all—would be a great way for God to get man's attention?

This is exactly what the Bible says God did to authenticate His message and messengers.

"Men of Israel, hear these words: Jesus of Nazareth, a man attested to you by God with mighty works and wonders and signs that God did through him in your midst, as you yourselves know" (Acts 2:22, emphasis added).

—In comparing Jesus, Zoroaster, Buddha, Socrates and Muhammad, if we exclude later legendary and apologetic accounts, we find that early accounts attribute miracles only to Jesus.‖ Edwin M. Yamauchi, Professor Emeritus of history at Miami University "Historical Notes on the (In)comparable Christ," in Christianity Today, October 22, 1971, pp. 7-11, http://www.irr.org/yamauchi.html (emphasis added)

—But if we admit God, must we admit miracles? Indeed, indeed you have no security against it. That is the bargain.‖ C.S. Lewis, Miracles, p. 109.

Conclusion – God exists; miracles are possible.

Can we Trust the Bible?

Is the New Testament Accurate?

The New Testament is accurate, according to most Biblical scholars. In the Baker Encyclopedia of Apologetics, 2002, Baker Books: Grand Rapids (MI), pp. 532- 533, Bruce Metzger, a highly recognized scholar, is quoted as estimating the New Testament we have today as 99.5 percent accurate to the original text.

There are approximately 5,700 handwritten manuscripts (MS) in Greek, which is the original language of the New Testament. In total, there are more than 25,000 full or partial manuscripts in several languages. Due to the enormous number of texts, giving more weight to the older manuscripts, scholars can compare one to another and determine what the originals said.

The texts have what scholars call variants: small variations, due to word placement (Jesus Christ vs. Christ Jesus, for example), spelling, proper nouns and the like. These are not errors, simply variations in the text. Because there are more than 25,000 manuscripts, there are an estimated 400,000 variants. Here are two simulated verses that vary in four places, thus five variants:

Jesus Christ died for our sin and rose again.

Christ Jesus died for your sins and arose.

The actual texts have nowhere near this number per line. If 1,000 manuscripts had 100 spelling errors each, that would equal 100,000 variants. This demonstrates why the estimated 400,000 variants discovered in the manuscripts are not that significant. Notice how even in a short verse with several variants, we can still determine what the verse says. If you had 1,000 MS with the same verse, do you think you could figure out what it says?

According to Biblical scholars, inconsequential variants like these alter no meaning and account for 99 percent of the total. Only one percent of variants are of any consequence, and they do not affect Christian doctrine. Ironically, God's plan for man to disperse thousands of handwritten manuscripts in the ancient world protected it from alteration better than if one person had the original and could change it.

—While the New Testament documents do not survive or have not yet been found, we have abundant and accurate copies of the original New Testament documents – many more than for the ten best pieces of ancient literature combined. Moreover, nearly perfect reconstruction of the originals can be accomplished by comparing the thousands of manuscript copies that do survive. We have discovered manuscript fragments from the second century and as early as the mid-first century. There are no works from the ancient world that even come close to the New Testament in terms of manuscript support.‖ Turek and Geisler, I Don't Have Enough Faith to Be an Atheist, page 248.

Non-believers are concerned that our New Testament Scriptures cannot be trusted, but they've come to this concern without examining the evidence. As Christians, we KNOW that we have the most reliable and attested ancient documents. You can trust that, if nothing else, we have today what the ancients had to begin with.‖ Detective Jim Wallace, former atheist, www.pleaseconvinceme.com

—In addition to all of the manuscripts, there are more than 36,000 instances of quotation of New Testament scriptures by the early church fathers. All but eleven New Testament verses are quoted, allowing for virtually 100 percent reconstruction of the New Testament.‖ Norman Geisler and William Nix, General Introduction to the Bible (Chicago: Moody, 1986), 431.

All Scripture is breathed out by God and profitable for teaching, for reproof, for correction, and for training in righteousness (2 Tim. 3:16).

Knowing this first of all, that no prophecy of Scripture comes from someone's own interpretation. For no prophecy was ever produced by the will of man, but men spoke from God as they were carried along by the Holy Spirit (2 Peter 1:20- 21).

—The interval between the dates of original composition (of the N.T.) and the earliest extant evidence becomes so small as to be in fact negligible and the foundation for any doubt that the Scriptures have come down to us substantially as they were written has now been removed; both the authenticity and the general integrity of the books of the N.T. may be regarded as firmly established.‖ Sir Frederic Kenyon, Director, principal librarian of the British museum, foremost expert on ancient manuscripts.

—The science of textual criticism is used to test all documents of antiquity--not just religious texts--including historical and literary writings. It's not a theological enterprise based on haphazard hopes and guesses; it's a linguistic exercise that follows a set of established rules. Textual criticism allows an alert critic to determine the extent of possible corruption of any work. ‖ Greg Koukel, Host of Stand to Reason radio program since 1990, Los Angeles, CA, www.str.org

Conclusion – Most Biblical scholars agree that we have an accurate copy of the entire Bible.

Is the New Testament True?

Five compelling points say that the New Testament is true.

1. Prophetic Testimony

Many consider the approximately 2,000 Old Testament prophecies discovered to date to be God's fingerprints. Over 300 of them predicted a Messiah who would come, and these were written more than 400 years before the birth of Jesus. They precisely match Jesus' life, death and resurrection. Consider the following fifteen prophesies:

Prophecy	Prophesied	Fulfilled
Born of a virgin	Isa. 7:14	Matt. 1:18, 25
Born in Bethlehem	Micah 5:2	Matt. 2:1
Preceded by a messenger	Isa. 40:3	Matt. 3:1-2
Rejected by His own people	Isa. 53:3	John 7:5; 7:48
Betrayed by a close friend	Psalm 41:9	John 13:26-30
His side pierced	Zech. 12:10	John 19:34
Crucifixion	Psalm 22:1, 11-18	Luke 23:33
Will pray for His persecutors	Isa. 53:12	Luke 23:34
Friends, family will witness	Psalm 38:11	Luke 23:49

Garments divided, casting lots	Psalm 22:18	John 19:23-24
Will be given gall and vinegar	Psalm 69:21	Matt. 27:34
Will commit Himself to God	Psalm 31:5	Luke 23:46
Bones will be left unbroken	Psalm 34:20	John 19:33
Heart will rupture	Psalm 22:14	John 19:34
Resurrection	Psalm 16:10	Acts 13:34-37

—Peter Stoner considered the mathematical odds of one person meeting only eight prophecies and ruled out coincidence by the science of probability. We find that the chance that any man might have lived down to the present time and fulfilled all eight prophecies is one in ten to the seventeenth power. That's one in 100,000,000,000,000,000. Stoner illustrates it by supposing that we take 100,000,000,000,000,000 silver dollars and lay them on the face of Texas. They will cover all of the state two feet deep. Now mark one of these silver dollars and stir the whole mass thoroughly, all over the state. Blindfold a man and tell him that he can travel as far as he wishes, but he must pick up one silver dollar and say that this is the right one. What chance would he have of getting the right one? Just the same chance that the prophets would have had of writing these eight prophecies and having them all come true in any one man. Stoner considers forty-eight prophecies (of the 300 plus) and reports; _We find the chance that any one man fulfilled all forty-eight prophecies to be one in ten to the 157th power.' That is one chance in one with 157 zeros after it.ll Peter Stoner in Science Speaks, quoted from The New Evidence that Demands a Verdict, p 193, author, speaker Josh McDowell, www.josh.org

Were the Prophecies Written Before Jesus?

That is a very important question. The experts in the field of manuscript dating place the writings of the Old Testament books from 1445 B.C. to 425 B.C. (B.C. means before Christ). Scholars date the crucifixion to about A.D. 33 (A.D. means anno domini, year of our Lord, and in A.D. 33, Jesus was 32-33 years old). The facts indicate that all of the Old Testament prophecies were written hundreds of years prior to Jesus' birth.

One of the earliest manuscript discoveries is a complete 24-foot Isaiah scroll dated before 100 B.C. It is part of the Dead Sea Scrolls and any reputable scholar will tell you the evidence is clear that it existed before Jesus' birth, yet it describes Him in detail.

But he was wounded for our transgressions; he was crushed for our iniquities; upon him was the chastisement that brought us peace, and with his stripes we are healed. All we like sheep have gone astray; we have turned—every one—to his own way; and the Lord has laid on him the iniquity of us all (Isa. 53:5-6).

The New Testament writers and Jesus use the words —it is written‖ (referring to the Old Testament scriptures) seventy-two times in the English Standard Version (ESV) of the New Testament. Jesus actually quoted from or referred to twenty-four of the books of the Old Testament, including the book of Isaiah. The facts are clear that the Old Testament books were written prior to Jesus' birth.

Another prophecy, in Isaiah chapter seven, states that a virgin will give birth and they will call Him Immanuel, which means God with us.

Therefore the Lord himself will give you a sign: The virgin will be with child and will give birth to a son, and will call him Immanuel (Isa. 7:14).

In chapter nine of Isaiah, there is further information to pinpoint the child and reveal His identity. He will be born of a virgin and His name shall be called Mighty God and Everlasting Father. Jesus is the only one who can fit these prophecies.

For to us a child is born, to us a son is given; and the government shall be upon his shoulder, and his name shall be called Wonderful Counselor, Mighty God, Everlasting Father, Prince of Peace (Isa. 9:6, emphasis added).

―The Septuagint and the Dead Sea Scrolls establish a very dramatic piece of evidence for Christianity—that the Old Testament prophecies of the coming Messiah unquestionably predated the time that Jesus Christ walked the Earth. All theories of First Century A.D. conspiracies and prophecy manipulation go out the door when we realize that prophetic scripture like Isaiah 53 and Psalm 22 were fixed in written form at least 100 years before Christ, and probably many more.‖ www.septuagint.net

―The world would have us believe that our scriptures have been corrupted over time, but the evidence is clear here. Don't be fooled. More scholarship has been spent on this singular issue than on perhaps any other studies of ancient documents. Let the world think what it may; we can be confident in the knowledge that the Old Testament is true to its history and amazingly accurate.‖ Detective Jim Wallace, www.pleaseconvinceme.com (emphasis added).

Robert Dick Wilson, a Biblical scholar who is fluent in more than forty-five languages and dialects, concluded the following after a lifetime study of the Old Testament: ―I may add that the result of my 45 years of study of the Bible has led me all the time to a firmer faith that, in the Old Testament, we have a true historical account of the history of the Israelite people.‖ http://encycl.opentopia.com/term/Robert_Dick_Wilson

Prophecy in Our Generation

While we are on the subject, I want to point out four specific prophecies made thousands of years ago. The Bible indicates that the first three, which have been fulfilled, will be a sign that the second return of Jesus is not far off. The fourth one is where Jesus predicts His return, yet to come.

1. The gathering of the Jews into their homeland (Eze. 34:13).

2. The rebirth of Israel in a single day (Isa. 66:8-9). This occurred in 1948, almost two thousand years after the Jews lost their nation in A.D. 70.

3. The nations of the earth aligned against Israel (Zech. 12:2-3).

4. Jesus' future return to judge the living and the dead (Matt. 24:29-3). No one knows the time (Matt. 24:36-37).

Consider these prophecies that are being fulfilled before our very eyes, with a warning about counterfeit Christs and false prophets included:

"Tell us, when will these things be, and what will be the sign of your coming and of the close of the age?" And Jesus answered them, "See that no one leads you astray. For many will come in my name, saying, „I am the Christ," and they will lead many astray. And you will hear of wars and rumors of wars. See that you are not alarmed, for this must take place, but the end is not yet. For nation will rise against nation, and kingdom against kingdom, and there will be famines and earthquakes in various places" (Matt. 24:3-7).

For people will be lovers of self, lovers of money, proud, arrogant, abusive, disobedient to their parents, ungrateful, unholy heartless, unappeasable, slanderous, without self-control, brutal, not loving good, treacherous, reckless, swollen with conceit, lovers of pleasure rather than lovers of God (2 Tim. 3:2-4).

Conclusion – 300 specific prophecies about Jesus written 400 or more years before His birth precisely reveal that Jesus is the Messiah.

2. Embarrassing Testimony

The —Principle of Embarrassmentǁ is one method used by historians to decide if the authors of a text are telling the truth. This principle says that if the text is embarrassing to the author or authors, it is probably true. This is because people do not fabricate events that make them look bad. As a matter of fact, they may leave such events out, in an attempt to look good.

Consider what a person who is trying to sell you a lie might do. Let's say a man wanted you to invest your life savings with him. What kind of picture would he paint with the words and literature he offers? No problems, right? Consider if the writers of the Bible were trying to make up a God they wanted you to believe in. Wouldn't they do the same and claim there were no problems? Yet the Bible is filled with embarrassing details about Jesus and the disciples. His followers had many of the same problems we see Christians struggling with today. Experts say embarrassing testimony like this would be counterproductive in a plot to falsely claim that Jesus is God. Therefore, the following embarrassing details about what some thought of Jesus could only be a true report of what actually happened. This supports the belief that the disciples told the unvarnished truth. Note that the following claims are not supported by facts. They are simply a reporting of what some people, mainly Jesus detractors, claimed.

Called a drunkard - John 10:19 Called a madman - John 10:20

His family thinks he is out of his mind – Mark 3:21

Not believed by his brothers - John 7:5

Called demon-possessed - Mark 3:22, John 7:20, 8:48 Thought to be a deceiver - John 7:12

Deserted by many followers - John 6:66

Crucified despite the belief that anyone hung on a tree is cursed, making it very difficult for Jews to accept – Deut. 21:23

―People do not make up embarrassing details about themselves.‖ Dr. Frank Turek. Embarrassing testimony support adapted from Turek & Geisler's I Don't Have Enough Faith to Be an Atheist.

Conclusion – If you were making up a God you wanted everyone to believe in, you would not include embarrassing details, especially about Jesus, unless it was a true reporting of what happened.

3. Early Testimony

If you were reading a history book about Iraq and Saddam Hussein and there was no mention of the U.S. invasion and the fall of Hussein's dictatorship, would you think the book was written before or after the event happened? The most reasonable answer would be that it was written before the U.S. invasion, since there was no mention of it in the book.

There are two established historical events that virtually all scholars agree on: the crucifixion of Jesus in about A.D. 33 and the destruction of the Jewish temple in

A.D. 70. In A.D. 66 – 70, the Jews lost their homeland when the Romans overran the nation of Israel, destroyed the Jewish temple and killed or took into captivity over a million Jews. This cataclysmic event is never mentioned in the New Testament, except when Jesus predicts it in Matthew 24:2. Many scholars believe that if Jesus' prediction of this vast devastation had come true prior to when the New Testament was written, it would have strengthened the case for Christianity to have mentioned that His prediction had been fulfilled. Since it is not recorded, it is quite probable that most if not all of the New Testament was written prior to the temple's destruction in A.D. 66-70. This places all of the New Testament writings within thirty-seven years of the resurrection.

—There is a growing acceptance of earlier New Testament dates, even among critical scholars like John A.T. Robinson known for launching the _Death of God' movement. He wrote in his book Re-dating the New Testament dates placing the documents earlier than any conservative scholar ever held, and he concluded that one or two of the gospels could have been written as early as seven years after the crucifixion. At the latest, they were all composed in the lifetime of the eyewitnesses.‖ Dr. Norman Geisler, speaker, author or editor of over 60 books, Baker Encyclopedia of Apologetics.

—In my opinion, every book of the New Testament was written by a baptized Jew between the 40's and the 80's of the first century (very probably sometime between A.D. 50 and 70).‖ William F, Albright a foremost biblical archeologist, Christianity Today #7.

—Since the New Testament documents are referenced by other writers by about A.D. 100, they had to have been composed before then.‖ Turek and Geisler, I Don't Have Enough Faith to Be an Atheist, page 249.

Conclusion – Strong evidence suggests that most if not all of the New Testament was written before A.D. 70, during the lifetime of the eyewitnesses.

4. Eyewitness Testimony

The disciples gave up their lives for what they claimed. Multiple eyewitness accounts of something yesterday or 2,000 years ago are still valid. One way to determine if we can trust their eyewitness claims is to see if they were telling the truth in other areas we can verify. If we find their writings are fabricated points thrown together, we might not need to look further.

Read the following as it attests to the accuracy and truthfulness of the Bible.

In the fifteenth year of the reign of Tiberius Caesar, Pontius Pilate being governor of Judea, and Herod being tetrarch of Galilee, and his brother Philip tetrarch of the region of Ituraea and Trachonitis, and Lysanias tetrarch of Abilene, during the high priesthood of Annas and Caiaphas, the word of God came to John the son of Zechariah in the wilderness (Luke 3:1-2).

1. An exact date is given.

2. All eight people are known from history.

3. All were known to live at this exact time.

Luke wrote the books of Luke and Acts. From Acts, eighty-four historical details have been confirmed. Luke also reports over thirty-five miracles in Acts. The New Testament names more than thirty people who are confirmed to have lived by secular sources or archeology. The book of John has fifty-nine verified historical details, according Geisler and Turek in I Don't Have Enough Faith to Be Atheist.

—Luke is a historian of first rank. This author should be placed along with the greatest of historians.‖ Sir William Ramsey, archeologist, The Bearing of Recent Discovery on the Trustworthiness of the New Testament.

Knowing that the disciples were taught by Jesus (a man renowned for His honesty) and that everything we can verify to this point indicates the disciples have been completely truthful, should they be given the benefit of the doubt with their eyewitness reports of miracles, including the resurrection? There is no question that the disciples believe they saw the resurrected Jesus several times over forty days. They wanted you to believe, too, and this explains their meticulous fact reporting. Here are a few of many verses wherein they claim to be eyewitnesses.

And you killed the Author of life, whom God raised from the dead. To this we are witnesses (Acts 3:15, emphasis added).

He who saw it has borne witness—his testimony is true, and he knows that he is telling the truth—that you also may believe (John 19:35, emphasis added).

That which was from the beginning, which we have heard, which we have seen with our eyes, which we looked upon and have touched with our hands, concerning the word of life— the life was made manifest, and we have seen it, and testify to it and proclaim to you the eternal life, which was with the Father and was made manifest to us (1 John 1:1-2, emphasis added).

For we did not follow cleverly devised myths when we made known to you the power and coming of our Lord Jesus Christ, but we were eyewitnesses of his majesty (2 Peter 1:16, emphasis added).

Criminal investigators often state that the testimonies at crime scenes can sometimes seem like the witnesses saw different crimes, but the details are frequently complementary, not contradictory.

—Minor differences in multiple eyewitness accounts are normal and jury instructions advise jurors to be aware of this fact. Did the

58

witness's testimony differ from the testimony of other witnesses? When weighing the conflicting testimony, you should consider whether the discrepancy has to do with a material fact or with an unimportant detail.‖ Criminal Pattern Jury Instruction, US Court of Appeals for the Tenth Circuit 2005 Ed.

In the next five verses, which many critics accept as being written within three to five years of the resurrection, the apostle Paul lists the eyewitnesses:

For I delivered to you as of first importance what I also received: that Christ died for our sins in accordance with the Scriptures, that he was buried, that he was raised on the third day in accordance with the Scriptures, and that he appeared to Cephas (Peter), then to the twelve. Then he appeared to more than five hundred brothers at one time, most of whom are still alive, though some have fallen asleep. Then he appeared to James, then to all the apostles. Last of all, as to one untimely born, he appeared also to me (1 Cor. 15:3-8).

—If we are looking honestly at any event in ancient history, we are going to have to trust the ancient written record and the supporting archeology. We need to evaluate them as we would any other set of witnesses. The Biblical eyewitnesses DO measure up under these standards. They wrote within close proximity to the life of Jesus, their testimony is supported externally by the archeological evidence, they have a reliable track record (also supported by the archeology) and they are without ulterior motive. While many would argue that we have to account for the life of Jesus purely OUTSIDE the Biblical record in order to be confident that we have the unbiased truth, we need to remember that the Bible itself is a reliable and trustworthy eyewitness account.‖ Jim Wallace, Cold Case Homicide Detective, former atheist, www.pleaseconvinceme.com

—How do we explain the fact that this movement spread like wildfire with Jesus as the Messiah, even though Jesus had been crucified? The answer has to be, it can only be, because He was raised from the dead.‖ N.T. Wright, Professor of NT studies, Oxford, video documentary, The Search Continues, www.johnankerburg.org

—Are these men (Jesus and the disciples), who helped to transform the moral structure of society, consummate liars or deluded madmen? These alternatives are harder to believe than the fact of the resurrection, and there is no shred of evidence to support them.‖ Paul Little, Know Why You Believe, Wheaton, IL, Scripture Press.

5. Would You Die for a Lie, Knowing it was a Lie?

I think we can all agree that if the message in the New Testament presented by the disciples was a lie, they knew it, since they would have been the ones to make it up. While a young terrorist might die for something he believes is true, people do not die for something they know for certain is a lie. The disciples claimed to be eyewitnesses to the resurrection of Jesus. Even if they had never written a word, the testimony they gave with their lives and their deaths speaks volumes. The following indicates the ultimate price each paid. The amount of evidence for each apostle's death varies. Some are reported in the Bible. Some are from early church fathers and other historical writings.

Peter was crucified head down in Rome in 66 A.D.
Andrew was crucified A.D. 74.

James, son of Zebedee, beheaded by a sword (Acts 12:1-9).
John was banished to the Isle of Patmos in A.D. 96 (Rev. 1- 9).
Phillip was crucified at Heirapole, Phrygia in A.D. 52.
Bartholomew was beaten, crucified, and beheaded in A.D. 52.
Thomas was run through by a lance in East Indies in A.D. 52.

Matthew, stoned and slain by a sword Ethiopia about A.D. 60.
James, son of Alphaeus, was beaten to death in A.D. 60
Thaddeus was shot to death by arrows in A.D. 72.
Simon was crucified in Persia in A.D. 74.
Paul was beheaded in Rome in mid-A.D. 60's.

FOXE'S BOOK OF MARTYRS,
http://www.ccel.org/f/foxe/martyrs/fox101.htm

Could you get eleven of your friends to make up a huge lie and walk away from their careers, religious beliefs, friends and families to tell the world that lie, for no worldly gain? What if you offered them the bonus of persecution, torture and a brutal death? No one in their right mind would do that. But this is exactly what anyone would need to believe if they claim the disciples made up the resurrection.

The disciples had no reason to make up a new religion. As Jews, they already thought they were God's chosen people. If Judaism were true, as they had always been taught, they would be condemned for this change in belief. The only real option is that the disciples were telling the truth and it was so significant that they refused to deny it.

They were stoned, they were sawn in two, they were killed with the sword. They went about in skins of sheep and goats, destitute, afflicted, mistreated—Heb 11:37

—People die for a lie they believe is true all of the time but no one dies for a lie they know is a lie.‖ Dr. Frank Turek, www.Crossexamined.org

—The power of the Biblical record is that the Biblical eyewitnesses had NO positive motive for their story except for the fact that it was TRUE. They gained no wealth, no comfortable lifestyle, and no assurance of a painless death. Witnesses without a positive motive other than truth are THE best witnesses in the world. When you see them suffering for their testimony, you can be sure you are hearing the truth.‖ Jim Wallace, Cold Case Homicide Detective, a former atheist, www.pleaseconvinceme.com

—Why would they die for what they knew to be a lie? A person might be deceived and die for a falsehood. But the apostles were in a position to know the facts about Jesus's resurrection, and they still died for it.‖ History Professor Lynn Gardner, Christianity Stands True, College Press, 1994.

Conclusion – People do not die for a lie they know for a fact is a lie. The disciples told the truth about the resurrection of Jesus.

What About the Old Testament?

Based on the following statistics, it is clear that Jesus and the writers of the New Testament believed the Old Testament was true.

1. Roger Nicole maintains that the number of quotations and references in the New Testament to the Old Testament may be as high as 4,105. The Expositor's Bible Commentary, 1979, Vol. I, p. 617

2. Jesus quoted from twenty-four different Old Testament books, affirming as true some of the most attacked events in the Old Testament. The events Jesus affirmed include the following: Creation (Mark 13:19), Noah and the flood (Matt. 24:39), Adam and Eve (Matt.19:4-5), Sodom and Gomorrah (Luke - 10:12), Moses and the burning bush (Luke 20:37), and Jonah and the great fish (Matt.12:40). In Matthew 23, using the first and last prophets as bookends, Jesus confirmed the validity of the entire Old Testament by saying, —From the blood of Abel to that of

Zechariah.‖ Jewish New Testament Publications, Jerusalem, 1989. home.comcast.net/~StudyTheBible/InfoJewish.rtf

Does Archaeology Support the Bible?

There are thousands of historical facts in the Bible that have been confirmed by archaeology.

"It may be stated categorically that no archaeological discovery has ever invalidated a Biblical reference. Scores of archaeological findings have been made which confirm in clear outline or exact detail historical statements in the Bible. And, by the same token, proper evaluation of Biblical description has often led to amazing discoveries." Dr. Nelson Glueck, Rivers in the Desert.

—I know of no finding in archaeology that's properly confirmed which is in opposition to the Scriptures. The Bible is the most accurate history textbook the world has ever seen.‖ Dr. Clifford Wilson, former director Australian Institute of Archaeology, radio interview by the Institute for Creation Research, ICR radio transcript No 0279-1004.

—It is important to remember when comparing archaeology to the Bible, that the Bible is itself an archaeological document of the highest caliber...Of all the documents known to man, only the Hebrew-Greek Scriptures have certified their accuracy and divine authority by a pattern of prediction and fulfillment completely beyond the capabilities of man and possible only for God.‖ Archer, The Encyclopedia of Bible Difficulties.

"There can be no doubt that archaeology has confirmed the substantial historicity of Old Testament tradition." Dr. William F. Albright, Archaeology and the Religions of Israel.

Do any Non-Christian Writings Support the Bible?

Most people are not even aware of non-Christian writings and how they firmly support the testimony in the New Testament. According to Biblical scholar Gary Habermas, there are seventeen secular writings, all written within 150 years of the resurrection, which offer evidence as to the reliability of the events of the New Testament. Here are three:

"At this time there was a wise man who was called Jesus. Pilate condemned Him to be condemned and to die. And those who had become His disciples did not abandon His discipleship. They reported that He had appeared to them three days after His crucifixion and that He was alive; accordingly, He was perhaps the Messiah concerning whom the prophets have recounted wonders." Josephus (A.D.37 – 100) the greatest Jewish historian of the first century, Antiquities of the Jews, xviii.ch. 3, subtopic 3, Arabic text.

"[Christians] were in the habit of meeting on a certain fixed day before it was light, when they sang in alternate verse of a hymn to Christ as to a god, and bound themselves to a solemn oath, not to do any wicked deeds, and never to deny a truth when they should be called upon to deliver it up." Pliny the Younger A.D.

112, Epistles, X.96, a letter he wrote to Emperor Trajan asking how to punish Christians for their belief.

"Hence to suppress the rumor, he falsely charged with the guilt, and punished with the most exquisite tortures, the persons commonly called Christians, who were hated for their enormities. Christus (same as Christ), the founder of the name, was put to death by Pontius Pilate, procurator of Judea in the reign of Tiberius: but the pernicious superstition, repressed for a time broke out again, not only through Judea, where the mischief originated, but through the city of Rome also." Tacitus (A.D. 56-

A.D. 120), Roman Historian, Annals XV.44, written of Nero's attempt to relieve himself of burning Rome by blaming it on Christians.

The following compilation of these writings from Detective Jim Wallace's website is a list of the facts taken from these seventeen secular sources. I have divided up compilations numerically, so it is easier to read. As you read, you need to take into account that these sources were watching from a distance. Therefore, they did not know exactly what was happening. So, for example, they use the word magic instead of miracles. The point is that these writings match numerous specific details reported in the New Testament. This is additional validation that the testimony in the New Testament is a true reporting of what transpired.

1) Jesus was born and lived in Palestine.

2) He was born, supposedly, to a virgin and had an earthly father who was a carpenter.

3) He was a teacher who taught that by repentance and belief, all followers would become brothers and sisters.

4) He led the Jews away from their beliefs.

5) He was a wise man who claimed to be God and the Messiah.

6) He had unusual magical powers and performed miraculous deeds.

7) He healed the lame.

8) He accurately predicted the future.

9) He was persecuted by the Jews for what he said and betrayed by Judah Iskarioto.

10) He was beaten with rods, forced to drink vinegar and wear a crown of thorns and crucified on the eve of the Passover.

11) His crucifixion occurred under the direction of Pontius Pilate, during the time of Tiberius.

12) On the day of his crucifixion, the sky grew dark and there was an earthquake. Afterward, he was buried in a tomb and the tomb was later found to be empty.

13) He appeared to his disciples resurrected from the grave and showed them his wounds.

14) These disciples then told others that Jesus was resurrected and ascended into heaven.

15) Jesus' disciples and followers upheld a high moral code.

16) One of them was named Matthai.

17) The disciples were also persecuted for their faith but were martyred without changing their claims.

18) They met regularly to worship Jesus, even after his death.

pleaseconvinceme.com/ and coldcasechristianity.com

Conclusion – The seventeen non-Christian writings confirm much of what is written in the New Testament. If Christianity were a myth or a made-up religion, these secular writings would not exist.

Is the Bible Filled with Contradictions?

This is a legitimate question, but the consensus from those who have diligently examined the Bible is no. Just as a detective might initially think there are contradictions between multiple eyewitness accounts of an event, upon further examination he may find that they are complementary, not contradictory.

To give you a firsthand example, near the beginning of this book I mention I have spoken to hundreds of people directly. On five other pages, I say thousands of people. If found in the Bible, skeptics would post it on their website and cry that it is a contradiction. Presented out of context, it does appear to be one. But if you look closely, you will see I stated —the hundreds of people I have asked this specific question.‖ In other words, I have spoken to thousands of people but only asked that specific question to hundreds. Thus, this supposed contradiction ends up being complementary, not contradictory, just as we see with multiple eyewitness testimonies to any event. Context is crucial when you are reading any book, but especially in a book with forty authors written over 1500 years.

Did the Resurrection Really Happen?

A Minimal Facts Argument for the Resurrection

Some of the strongest evidence we have seen for the resurrection is the willingness of the original disciples and the apostle Paul to die for their testimony that Jesus rose from the dead. We also have the non-Christian writings we reviewed that support the resurrection. Now we will review a consensus of 1,400 scholars.

The minimal facts approach to the resurrection was originated by biblical scholar Gary Habermas (garyhabermas.com). It is based on his research of 1,400 in-depth scholarly writings regarding the crucifixion and resurrection of Jesus. Dr.

Habermas relies only on those facts supported by multiple sources and accepted by the vast majority of scholars. The facts below, except the fourth one listed, are accepted by 95 to 100 percent of the 1,400 scholars. Number four is accepted by about 75 percent:

1. Jesus died by crucifixion.

2. He was buried.

3. His death caused the disciples to despair and lose hope.

4. The tomb where He had been buried was found empty.

5. The disciples claim appearances of the risen Jesus.

6. The disciples changed from doubters to bold witnesses.

7. The resurrection was the central message.

8. Preached the message of resurrection in Jerusalem.

9. The Church was born and grew.

10. Christian Jews made Sunday primary day of worship.

11. James believed when he saw resurrected Jesus

12. Paul converted to the faith (Paul was an enemy).

Minimal facts argument by Biblical Scholar and author Gary Habermas. www.garyhabermas.com

The fact that such a large percentage of scholars accepts these twelve points is quite compelling. One thing is certain: Jesus existed. When it comes to number four, the empty tomb, there is some disagreement about why it was empty and if Jesus did, in fact, rise from the dead. As you review the following six possibilities offered through the years, consider which one you believe offers the best explanation. Keep in mind that the facts indicate God exists; therefore, miracles cannot be ruled out.

1. Hallucination Theory

The problem with this theory is that Jesus appeared to more than 500 people, in different locations and circumstances (eating, walking, talking, etc.), over forty days. Hallucinations do not repeatedly happen to different groups of people for extended periods. The resurrected Jesus even told Thomas to touch him.

Then He (Jesus) said to Thomas, "Put your finger here, and see my hands; and put out your hand, and place it in my side. Do not disbelieve, but believe" (John 20:27, emphasis added).

Not to all the people but to us who had been chosen by God as witnesses, who ate and drank with him after he rose from the dead (Acts 10:41, emphasis added).

And He (Jesus) said to them, "Why are you troubled, and why do doubts arise in your hearts? See my hands and my feet, that it is I myself. Touch me, and see. For a spirit does not have flesh and bones as you see that I have" (Luke 24:28-39, emphasis added).

2. The Witness Went to the Wrong Tomb Theory

If this was true, the Romans who had posted guards at the actual tomb could have produced the body to stop Christianity cold, but they never even suggested the possibility. If you saw a loved one's body placed in a tomb, do you think you would forget the location three days later?

3. Swoon or Apparent Death Theory

This theory says the whipping, beating and crucifixion of Jesus did not kill Him and not even his professional executioners realized it. Then His disciples mistook a severally beaten Jesus, who would have been in desperate need of a doctor, for the risen Christ. Common sense and this testimony from medical experts disagree.

—Clearly the weight of historical and medical evidence indicates that Jesus was dead before the wound to his side was inflicted and supports the traditional view that the spear, thrust between his right ribs, probably perforated not only the right lung but also the pericardium and heart and thereby ensured his death.

Accordingly, interpretations based on the assumption that Jesus did not die on the cross are at odds with modern medical knowledge. ‖ William D. Edwards, Wesley J. Gabel and Floyd E. Hosmer, —On the Physical Death of Jesus Christ,‖ Journal of the American Medical Assoc., p. 255.

4. Someone Else was Crucified in Place of Jesus

This is what Islam claims, but there is no evidence to support it. Mary, Jesus' mother, was standing at the foot of the cross with John. Peter saw Him arrested and taken before Pilate, beaten and led off to be crucified. The Bible records others who knew Him and saw what was happening, including Nicodemus, who placed His body in the tomb. Don't you think someone would have said, —They killed the wrong guy?‖

5. The Disciples Stole the Body

This is the only explanation the Bible says the Jewish leaders offered for the empty tomb, and in doing so, they admitted the tomb was empty. But think about it—if the disciples stole the body, we are right back to the premise that they snuck by the posted Roman guards, rolled back the two-ton stone without the guards noticing, and made the entire resurrection story up to get themselves martyred. If this were the case, they died for what they knew was a lie.

6. Jesus Rose From the Dead

Numerous scholars believe this offers the best explanation. The main reason someone might reject this option is their prior rejection of miracles. But since the facts indicate God exists, miracles like the resurrection are definitely possible.

—You may be surprised to learn that the majority of New Testament critics investigating the gospels in this way accept the central facts undergirding the resurrection of Jesus. I want to emphasize that I am not talking about evangelical or conservative scholars only, but about the broad spectrum of New Testament critics who teach at secular universities and non-evangelical seminaries. Amazing as it may seem, most of them have come to regard as historical the basic facts which support the resurrection of Jesus‖. Christian Philosopher and Theologian Dr. William Lane Craig, www.reasonablefaith.org

—I say unequivocally that the evidence for the resurrection of Jesus Christ is so overwhelming that it compels acceptance by proof which leaves absolutely no room for doubt.‖ Sir Lionel Luckhoo, won 245 murder acquittals in a row, most successful lawyer in the world, according to The Guinness book of World Records. God's Outrageous Claims, Lee Strobel.

—Only Jesus predicted he would be resurrected after his death, and only his followers rest their faith on such an event. Jesus' death on the cross is unique not only in its manner but also in its alleged redemptive meaning. Neither Zoroaster, Buddha, Socrates nor Muhammad claimed his death would save men from their sins.‖ Edwin M. Yamauchi, Professor Emeritus of history, Miami University, www.irr.org/yamauchi.html

Who Did Jesus Claim to Be?

The list of contradictory beliefs about God we reviewed earlier contain a number of contrary beliefs about Jesus' identity. Beliefs vary between a man, a good teacher, an angel and the Son of God, God in the flesh as claimed by Christianity. Now we will look at who Jesus Himself claimed to be:

1. Jesus Claimed to be God

In the Old Testament, God calls Himself —I Am.‖ In the New Testament, Jesus uses the same name; the Jews realized what He was saying and picked up rocks to stone Him because they knew He was claiming to be God.

God said to Moses, "I AM WHO I AM." And He said, "Say this to the people of Israel, I AM has sent me to you" (Exodus 3:14).

Jesus said to them, "Truly, truly, I say to you, before Abraham was, I Am," so they picked up stones to throw at him, but Jesus hid himself and went out of the temple (John 8:58-59).

2. Jesus Claimed to be the Object of Prayer

Jesus claimed to be the mediator between God and man, thus claiming to be God. How would you respond if I asked you to pray in my name? *"Whatever you ask in my name, this I will do, that the Father may be glorified in the Son" (John 14:13).*

3. Jesus Claimed to Forgive Sins

We can all forgive someone for sinning against us personally. But each of the numerous times Jesus forgave sins, He had just met the people and they had not sinned against Him personally. He was forgiving their sins against God, something only God can do.

"Son, your sins are forgiven." Now some of the scribes were sitting there, questioning in their hearts, "Why does this man speak like that? He is blaspheming! Who can forgive sins but God alone?" (Mark 2:5-7, emphasis added).

4. Jesus Claimed to be Worthy of Honor Due Only to God

The Father judges no one, but has given all judgment to the Son, that all may honor the Son, just as they honor the Father.

Whoever does not honor the Son does not honor the Father who sent him (John 5: 22-23).

5. Jesus Claimed to be the Long Awaited Messiah

The woman said to him, "I know that Messiah is coming (he who is called Christ). When he comes, he will tell us all things." Jesus said to her, "I who speak to you am he" (John 4:25-26).

Caiaphas asks Jesus, "Are you the Christ, the Son of the Blessed?" And Jesus said, "I am, and you will see the Son of Man seated at the right hand of Power, and coming with the clouds of heaven" (Mark 14:61-62).

6. Jesus Claimed to be Equal in Authority with God

"Heaven and earth will pass away, but my words will not pass away" (Matt. 24:35).

And Jesus came and said to them, "All authority in heaven and on earth has been given to me" (Matt. 28:18).

7. Jesus Claimed to be Yahweh (LORD)

In the Old Testament, God is referred to in many ways. In the New Testament, the same attributes are applied to Jesus, suggesting that He is God in the flesh.

Old Testament	Name	New Testament
Psalm 23:1	Shepherd	Heb. 13:20
Isa. 44:4	First and Last	Rev. 1:17
Isa. 40:28	Creator	Col. 1:16-17
Isa. 62:5	Bridegroom	Matt. 25:1
Ps. 27:1	Light	John 8:12

Isa. 43:11	Savior	John 4:42
Isa. 42:8	God's Glory	John 17:5
1 Sam. 2:6	Giver of Life	John 5:21
Deut. 32:4	Rock	1 Cor. 10:4
Joel 3:12	Judge	2 Cor. 5:10

Revelation tells us it is —The Revelation of Jesus Christ.‖ In Revelation 1:17-18, we see Jesus claiming to be the First and Last, an Old Testament title in Isaiah 44:6 reserved for God. He also says, —I was dead and behold, I am alive forevermore,‖ which only fits Jesus.

When I saw him, I fell at his feet as though dead. But he laid his right hand on me, saying, —Fear not, I am the first and the last, and the living one. I died, and behold I am alive forevermore, and I have the keys of Death and Hades‖ (Rev. 1:17-18).

8. Jesus Accepted Worship Nine Different Occasions

1) Mother of James and John – Matt. 20:20

2) Possessed man - Mark 5:6

3) A blind man - Matt. 28:17

4) Doubting Thomas - Jn. 20:28

5) The women at the tomb - Matt. 28:9

6) A Canaanite woman - Matt. 15:25

7) His disciples - Matt. 14:33

8) A healed leper - Matt. 8:2

9) A rich young ruler - Matt. 9:18

Jesus was also a rabbi, and the first duty of a rabbi is to point out blasphemy. Yet Jesus never rebuked anyone who worshiped Him, and even commended Thomas in John 20:29. In contrast, the apostle John tried to worship an angel in Revelation 22:9 and was rebuked. Jesus, on the other hand, accepts worship reserved for God alone. He was more than an angel.

9. Jesus Claimed to be One with God the Father

It is clear that the Jewish witnesses had no trouble figuring out that Jesus was claiming to be God. They did not believe He was God, so in the end they crucified Him for blasphemy (claiming to be God, using God's name in vain). If He was not God, they would have been right.

"I and the Father are one." The Jews picked up stones again to stone him. Jesus answered them, "I have shown you many good works from the Father; for which of them are you going to stone me?" The Jews answered him, "It is not for a good work that we are going to stone you but for blasphemy, because you, being a man, make yourself God" (John 10:30-33).

10. Jesus Called Himself the Son of Man

In the first verse below, —Son of Man‖ is the God figure in the Old Testament.

I saw in the night visions, and behold, with the clouds of heaven there came one like a son of man, and he came to the Ancient of Days and was presented before him. And to him was given dominion and glory and a kingdom, that all peoples, nations, and languages should serve him; his dominion is an everlasting dominion, which shall not pass away, and his kingdom one that shall not be destroyed (Dan. 7:13-14).

In John 8:28, as well as eighty-two other instances in the New Testament, Jesus calls himself the Son of Man.

So Jesus said to them, "When you have lifted up the Son of Man, then you will know that I am he, and that I do nothing on my own authority, but speak just as the Father taught me" (John 8:28).

No matter who you or anyone else in the popular culture think Jesus is, based on the evidence, it's ludicrous to say that Jesus never claimed to be God. Format adapted from Dr. Frank Turek's video series I Do Not Have Enough Faith to Be an Atheist.

—Additionally there is an enormous difference between who Jesus claimed to be when compared to other leaders of different beliefs. Jesus claimed to be able to forgive sin, He accepted worship numerous times, and He said He was the only way to the Father. Only Jesus claimed equality with a sole, supreme deity. According to E.O. James, an authority on comparative religions, nowhere else had it ever been claimed that a historical founder of any religion was the one and only supreme deity. Only Jesus spoke on his own unquestioned authority. Zoroaster and Muhammad acted as spokesmen for God, while Socrates and Buddha urged every man to consult his own conscience.‖ Edwin M. Yamauchi, Professor Emeritus of history, Miami University, http://www.irr.org/yamauchi.html (emphasis added).

—Indeed, it's shocking to me how much of Jesus' life can be established, including his radical personal claims, his crucifixion, his burial in a tomb, the discovery of his empty tomb, his post-mortem appearances, and his disciples' coming to believe suddenly and sincerely that God had raised him from the dead. We therefore have quite solid reasons for believing in Christ on the basis of the historical facts preserved about him in the gospels.‖ Dr. William Lane Craig, www.reasonablefaith.org (emphasis added).

Conclusion – Jesus' claim to be God is supported in many ways. He gave us the ultimate proof by rising from the dead as He predicted. Therefore, Jesus is God who came in the flesh.

But I Thought Jesus was the Son of God

He is the Son of God; He shares the nature of God with the Father and the Holy Spirit. This is what is called the Trinity—one God but in three distinct persons: Father, Son and Holy Spirit. A very simple but limited analogy that seems to help people understand the Trinity is H2O. It can be water, ice, or steam—but the nature of all three is H2O. It is the Father, Son and Holy Spirit—but the nature of all three is God. The Trinity is hard to fully comprehend, but it's not contradictory since there are not three Gods and one God at the same time.

Think of it this way. Are you just as human as your earthly father? Yes. So, why would you think that the only begotten Son of God would be any less God than His Father?

How Could Jesus be God and Man?

The Bible tells us Jesus was both a man and God incarnate: deity willingly clothed with humanity. When reading through the Bible, it is important to consider who is speaking and who the audience is. For example, many people who do not believe in the Bible claim that Jesus said, —God forgives‖ and think it applies to everyone. But in context, this is spoken only about those who have placed their faith in Jesus. The importance of context is obvious.

The question of how could Jesus be both God and man needs to be asked in two ways. Did Jesus get hungry? As God, no; as man, yes. Did Jesus get tired? As God, no; as man, yes. Did Jesus die? As God, no; as man, yes. Dr. William Lane Craig uses an analogy that utilizes the movie Avatar to explain the two natures of Jesus:

—I explained the doctrine of Christ's being one person who has two natures and used the movie Avatar to illustrate the doctrine ("Avatar" is another word for incarnation). The movie tells the story of Jake Sully, a disabled marine who becomes an avatar among a race of extra-terrestrials called the Na'vi. He becomes physically incarnated among them as one of them. At the same time he doesn't cease to be human. So Jake has both a human nature and a Na'vi nature. In the movie these two natures have strikingly different powers. If you were to ask, _Can Jake Sully run?' The answer would have to be, _Yes and no: yes, in his Na'vi nature but no, in his human nature.' I told the audience that if you can make sense of Avatar, you can make sense of Christ's incarnation. For in a similar way, Christ has both a divine nature and a human nature. These natures have different powers. In his human nature Christ experienced all the limitations intrinsic to human nature. But in his divine nature he had supernatural powers. Just as Jake Sully in his Na'vi nature became the Savior of the Na'vi people, so Christ in his human nature becomes the Savior of mankind.‖ William Lane Craig, Christian philosopher and theologian, debate with Yusuf Ismail, www.reasonablefaith.org

Transformed Lives

Some may consider the transformation of lives to be subjective evidence because it deals with personal experience. But based upon the incredible number of visibly changed lives and people who will personally attest to the presence of God's power in their life, I believe it is one of the most powerful pieces of evidence for Christianity.

I can personally confirm Jesus' transforming power in my own experience. There is nothing in this world like a personal relationship with Him. No matter what happens, He is always there for the believer as He promises in Hebrews 13:5: —... I will never leave you nor forsake you.‖ He fills the void we all have and

78

delivers a peace the world cannot hope to offer—peace with God and the hope of eternity without sorrow and pain. He loves us just as we are, and over time transforms us to become more like Him. Here are a few examples of transformed lives:

—I went to a motel on Christmas Eve; I intended to end my life. I lived most of my life out of control. I had used drugs and alcohol, I was put out of my home, and my wife told me to leave. As I am sitting in that room I noticed a book lying on top of the TV. I looked down and I saw that it was a Gideon Bible and I thought who needs that? I took my hand and I swiped it off onto the floor. Well it fell at my feet, but it fell open. What I read changed my life.‖ Elliot, video testimony from www.Gideons.org

—I picked up the Bible and I started reading. It was Romans 12:2, I'll never forget it. The verse says to not conform to the things of this world but be transformed by the renewal of your mind. For some reason something clicked. I have to renew my mind! If I renew my mind, then my actions will definitely follow.‖ Bradie James, NFL Dallas Cowboys, www.Iamsecond.com

—Being able to turn to Jesus during this crazy moment in my life gave me a sense of peace and confidence and I think that is just one thing that kept me alive.‖ Bethany Hamilton, on being able to turn to Jesus after a shark attack took her arm, www.Iamsecond.com

—I believe in Christ, I believe He's first in my life, family's second and everything else is after that. And I wouldn't be where I am today [without Him] because everything I tried to do on my own, well it almost cost me everything. So I put Christ first in my life today.‖ Josh Hamilton, Texas Rangers, www.Iamsecond.com

Lecrae was embroiled in a world filled with drugs, theft, alcohol and gang activity. —I didn't fit in anywhere. I was just a misfit of a person,‖ he said.

Little did he know that his view on life would soon be jolted, opening his eyes to the One who valued his life as significant. The One who cared enough to die for him. The One who is behind his music. LeCrae Moore, Christian rap artist, www.Iamsecond.com

Best Fits the Evidence

The following summary of conclusions is a logical argument for God's existence and identity. It follows the evidence to a final verdict:

1. Truth exists; its contradiction is always false.

2. The universe came into being out of nothing and requires a supernatural cause outside of itself.

3. The universe and life display highly complex design and require a highly intelligent designer. Life has only been observed coming from life.

4. The existence of the objective moral law, verified by our conscience, requires a moral lawgiver.

5. Points 2, 3 and 4 prove the absolute necessity of God's existence. Therefore God exists.

6. Since God exists, miracles are possible.

7. Based on manuscript evidence, the New Testament is 99 percent accurate.

8. Based on the facts, the New Testament, including the reports of the resurrection, is true.

9. The New Testament teaches that Jesus is God.

10. Jesus claimed to be God and verified it through miracles and the resurrection.

11. Therefore, Jesus is God.

12. Whatever God teaches is true.

13. Jesus taught the whole Bible is true.

14. Therefore, it is true that the Bible is the Word of God, and anything that contradicts it is false.

Points adapted and modified from Turek & Geisler video series/book I Do Not Have Enough Faith to Be an Atheist, p. 375

Conclusion – God exists, The Bible is true, and Jesus is God.

Your Verdict

I believe that the objective evidence strongly indicates that God exists and that Jesus is God in the flesh. But even in a jury trial with the most conclusive evidence, jurors do not always agree. This is your decision, and I want to make it crystal clear what you will be deciding. Imagine for a moment that you are seated on the jury in a crowded courtroom. All of the facts in the case have been presented, and in a few moments, you and the other jurors will begin your deliberation. As you get up to exit the courtroom, you intentionally take one last look at the defendant. Your gaze meets His as you notice His gentle smile and the love in His eyes. It is Jesus of Nazareth, a man acclaimed through the centuries for His honesty and ethical teaching. He professes to be God in the flesh. You suddenly realize that your decision ultimately comes down to whether or not you believe His claim. The facts support God's existence. Is Jesus the Son of God, God in the flesh?

Former atheist and author C.S Lewis was at one time in the same position you are in now. He believed Jesus' extraordinary claims eliminated the option that Jesus was just a good man or a good teacher. Therefore, only three possible options remain. As an argument coming from a once devout atheist who had no desire to believe in God, this quote is worth thoughtful consideration.

Lord, Liar, Lunatic

"I am trying here to prevent anyone saying the really foolish thing that people often say about Him: I'm ready to accept Jesus as a great moral teacher, but I don't accept his claim to be God. That is the one thing we must not say. A man who was merely a man and said the sort of things Jesus said would not be a great moral teacher. He would either be a lunatic — on the level with the man who says he is a poached egg—or else he would be the Devil of hell. You must make your choice. Either this man was, and is, the Son of God, or else a madman or something worse. You can shut him up for a fool, you can spit at him and kill him as a demon or you can fall at his feet and call him Lord and God, but let us not come with any patronizing nonsense about his being a great human teacher. He has not left that open to us. He did not intend to." C.S. Lewis, Mere Christianity.

The evidence convinced Lewis to set aside his pride, leave atheism and become a Christian. But it was not without an inner struggle. He even wrote a book called The Most Reluctant Convert where he admits that it was not in his plans to place his faith in Jesus. He could not deny the facts which revealed that Jesus is God. Lewis understood that the truth is often in opposition to our feelings. But he decided that the truth was the only place he wanted to reside, even though it meant humbling himself and changing his course in life.

Case Closed

Remember the story near the beginning of this book where six people claimed to be the sole heir to a fortune? When the investigation was complete and the truth was discovered, it was clear that the other five stories could not be true. If you believe the facts indicate that God exists and Jesus is God come in the flesh, examining every other belief would be futile. All other beliefs contradict the Bible, and therefore must be false. I have researched many other beliefs, and none offer anything remotely close to the verifiable historical facts Christianity offers. Furthermore, none have founders who claimed to be God and who proved it by rising from the dead. In our brief review, we have just scratched the surface of the vast amount of evidence which fits the God of the Bible like a glove. If anyone claims that another belief about God is true, ask them for the objective evidence.

So What?

Since we have discovered that the evidence supports the Bible as true, it only makes sense to investigate why Christians think it is so important, and how it applies to you personally. Before we start, you need to remember that the truth is what it is, whether we like it or not. This truth might initially be offensive and you may not immediately understand or accept it. But our next topic is the key to understanding the Gospel, which is the main message of the entire Bible.

The most common mistake that people make is thinking that their actions or good deeds are enough to get them into heaven. Most come to this conclusion through a comparison of themselves to other people, who they believe have committed bigger sins. If I stole once—so what? Someone else is a bank robber. If I lie, it's not all the time. If I go twelve miles per hour over the speed limit, it's okay because someone else is going twenty over. If I hide my income and lie to the IRS, others have done worse (and the IRS are crooks anyway).

Other times, people compare themselves to their past behavior and how much they have improved. I used to lie and steal, but now I do not. I used to drink and drive, but not now. I don't swear anymore. People tend to live by the rule well, at least I am not as bad as that guy to justify their sins. However, the Bible does not say that God grades on a curve by comparing us to others. His standard is perfection. The Bible warns against measuring ourselves by one another. When we do, it states that we will act without understanding. To act without understanding is to act foolishly.

Not that we dare to classify or compare ourselves with some of those who are commending themselves. But when they measure themselves by one another and compare themselves with one another, they are without understanding. 2 Cor 10:12

Consider this analogy:

Let's say you go to the doctor and you leave the exam room with the impression that you are healthy. As you leave, the nurse approaches you and hands you several medications for cancer. Would you take them? I wouldn't. Taking the medications without a diagnosis would be foolish.

The same truth applies to the gospel message, which can seem foolish without a true knowledge of our diagnosis before God. How do we obtain this diagnosis? In the following verse, the apostle Paul tells us. The knowledge of our sinful condition comes through our personal examination of God's law, not by comparing ourselves to other people or how we behaved in the past.

For by works of the law no human being will be justified in his sight, since through the law comes knowledge of sin (Rom. 3:20, emphasis added).

In essence, the law provides the diagnosis of our condition before a Holy, Just and Perfect God. In James 1:23-25, God's Law is compared to a mirror. We are concerned with our outward appearance, but God is concerned with what's inside as evidenced by our conscience. His law acts as a mirror reflecting what's in our hearts.

For the LORD sees not as man sees: man looks on the outward appearance, but the LORD looks on the heart (1 Sam. 16:7, emphasis added).

The following test is based on God's law and may seem harsh by humanity's low standard, but it will clearly diagnose your moral condition before a Holy God.

You are in the doctor's office again. The correct diagnosis, and therefore your life, depends on your truthfulness. For your benefit, set aside your pride, listen to your conscience and be totally honest before God. Admit to Him and yourself how many times you have broken the five commandments listed below (you can find the full Ten Commandments in Exodus 20).

Do You Think You Are a Good Person by God's Standard?

1. How many lies have you told in your life? (Exodus 20:16)

2. Have you ever stolen something, even as a child? Hid income to avoid taxes, illegally downloaded music or movies, taken items from work, been dishonest on an insurance claim? (Exodus 20:15)

3. Have you ever used God's name in vain? Using God's name frivolously or as a curse word is a form of blasphemy. (Exodus 20:7)

4. Have you committed adultery? Jesus said that just looking with sexual lust is adultery in God's eyes (Matt. 5:28). Ever done that?

5. Have you ever murdered anyone? Jesus said hate or strong dislike for someone qualifies as murder in God's eyes (Matt. 5:21-22). Ever done that?

Consider also any secret thing you have done in your life that you know God cannot condone. Listen to your conscience. God knows it all anyway.

Nothing is covered up that will not be revealed, or hidden that will not be known (Luke 12:2, emphasis added).

And no creature is hidden from his sight, but all are naked and exposed to the eyes of him to whom we must give account. (Heb. 4:13, emphasis added).

Once you see and accept the truth of your condition before God, your need for a Savior and the Gospel will make sense.

God Knows Our Thoughts.

By human standards, you and I might be able to say we are pretty good. But compared to God's standard of perfection, my conscience tells me I am a liar, thief, blasphemer, adulterer and a murderer at heart. What about you? If you have been honest, you know that God's law has just diagnosed your guilty condition before Him. If you are still minimizing and justifying your actions, think for a moment about how wrong you know it is when someone lies to or steals from you. Or how crazy it is to think God would allow unrepentant liars, thieves, blasphemers, adulterers or murderers into heaven. Since you are guilty, would you be headed to heaven or hell? Most people I speak to will admit that they are not headed to heaven, but a few are resistant. I like to ask them, —Do judges send the guilty to Disneyland, or do they go to prison?‖ The Bible warns us that God's prison is hell.

"Shame and everlasting contempt" Daniel 12:2 "Everlasting punishment" Matthew 25:46

"Indignation and wrath, tribulation and anguish" Romans 2:8,9

Considering the solid evidence for God and the Bible, does it concern you that the Bible states that if you died today without letting God save you, you would end up separated from God, in hell for eternity?

It should concern you greatly and it concerns God too. This is exactly why Jesus came: to save us from the condemnation our law-breaking has placed us under. God has not placed us under condemnation; we did it ourselves every time we rejected the advice from our conscience. Jesus came to save us from the consequences of our lawbreaking.

Most people have no objection to the thought of hell and punishment for murderers, rapists and serial killers. After all, who would expect God to welcome an unrepentant serial killer with open arms? However, hell for every unrepentant sinner makes sense, since the Bible states God is just and sin cannot go unpunished. It's not the existence of hell that most people have a problem with; it's who is going there. Yet, these same people will agree it makes perfect sense that God's standard would be much higher than human standards. Our conscience confirms this. By human standards, telling a lie is not that bad, but our God-given conscience disagrees. This is proof that God does not approve of telling lies. Conscience means with knowledge, so when we lie, we do it with knowledge that it's wrong. Like it or not, God's standard is much higher than ours. God is the Creator and we are the creation.

You turn things upside down! Shall the potter (Creator) be regarded as the clay (creation), that the thing made should say of its maker, "He did not make me;" or the thing formed say of him who formed it, "He has no understanding?" (Isa.29:16).

In Luke 13:3 and 5, Jesus, offers only two options—repent or perish. In other words, He is saying that God's perfect standard and the Gospel are the unchanging truth, whether we like it or not.

He is advising us to repent (change our mind) and believe His saving grace found only in the Gospel. He warns us if we do not, we will perish.

If the Bible is truth, God's moral law created for the greater good, just like the law of gravity, is not going to change because we believe something else. Violating God's moral law has real consequences, just like violating the law of gravity. We know that this is how truth works. God's plan, described in His Word, is simply a true explanation of the way it is. The next verses are Jesus speaking. I urge you to listen. These are not threats, they are God warning us. He is telling you to run to Him for safety from the wrath to come. The day when the world will be judged in perfect righteousness.

"... unless you repent, you will perish in the same way." (Luke 13:5, emphasis added).

"The time is fulfilled, and the kingdom of God is at hand; repent and believe in the gospel" (Mark 1:15, emphasis added).

Repent = Change Mind — Make the choice to change your mind from unbelief to belief. Accept God's truth as reality, humble yourself and turn to God, admit your sins, and throw yourself on God's grace and mercy, found only in Jesus Christ.

"For God so loved the world, that he gave his only Son, that whoever believes in him should not perish but have eternal life. For God did not send his Son into the world to condemn the world, but in order that the world might be saved through him. Whoever believes in him is not condemned, but whoever does not believe is condemned already, because he has not believed in the name of the only Son of God" (John 3:16-18, emphasis added).

"I tell you the truth, whoever hears my word and believes him who sent me has eternal life and will not be condemned; he has crossed over from death to life" (John 5:24, emphasis added).

"I told you that you would die in your sins, for unless you believe that I am he you will die in your sins" (John 8:24, emphasis added).

And from God the Father:

I call heaven and earth to witness against you today, that I have set before you life and death, blessing and curse. Therefore choose life, that you and your offspring may live, Deut 30:19

Why Did Jesus Come?

Notice in the following list how clear the message is. Jesus came to save the ungodly --the sinner -- and we all qualify.

To save sinners - 1 Tim. 1:15

To call sinners to repentance - Mark 2:17 To seek and save the lost - Luke 19:10

To give Himself as a ransom for sinners – Matt. 20:28

To die for the ungodly – Rom 5:6

To bear witness to the truth - John 18:37

To be a Light in the world - John 12:46

To proclaim and preach the Gospel - Mark 1:38 To die on the cross - John 12:27

To pay for our sins - 1 John 4:10

To be the Savior of the world - John-3:16-18 To redeem us from the law's curse – Gal. 4:4-5 To demonstrate God's love - 1 John 4:10

Objections

I have given the Good Person test directly to thousands of people, and I want to respond to a few of the objections I occasionally receive.

God forgives everyone. The Bible does not teach that everyone is forgiven, only those who change their mind from unbelief to belief. Once a person believes, they naturally flee to Jesus for safety from the day God will judge the world in righteousness. Jesus paid for our sins so we do not need to, so we can be forgiven.

I don't believe in hell. So what? The facts support the Bible. If it is true, it applies to you—whether you believe it or not. It is clear Jesus came to save us and he advises us to repent or perish. Even if we do not understand all of the consequences, isn't Jesus' sacrifice and warning enough to make you think? Why would Jesus do what he did if there were no consequences?

I do not want to believe in a God who would use fear to bring me to Him. The truth is, God loves you and is therefore warning you of what is certain to happen if you ignore or reject His counsel. If I took you to the top of the Empire State Building and hung you over the railing of the observation deck, would you refuse to respect gravity because you felt fear when you looked down? There are some things it makes sense to fear, and this knowledge has often kept you alive in your life. The Bible states:

The fear of the Lord is the beginning of knowledge; fools despise wisdom and instruction (Prov. 1:7).

Jesus goes against our natural inclination and, out of love, warns us to not even fear men who can kill us, in comparison to God who can take our life and cast us into hell.

"I tell you, my friends, do not fear those who kill the body, and after that have nothing more that they can do. But I will warn you whom to fear: fear him who, after he has killed, has authority to cast into hell. Yes, I tell you, fear him!" (Luke 12:4-5, emphasis added).

Think about the respectful fear you have for gravity every time you carefully approach the edge of a cliff or look over the railing of a high balcony. This is an indication of how we need to respect the Creator of gravity, God. This is the type of fear Jesus is speaking of when He says to fear God, the Creator of the universe. He holds our forgiveness in His hand. The good news is that the Bible also says God loves you and desires to save you from the condemnation your sin has placed you under. If you do feel fear, let it motivate you. Change your mind and run to God, the only one who can save and protect you.

The Bible tells us the good news—God wants to save you. God even tells us to choose life and not death. He is for you and not against you.

Who desires all people to be saved and to come to the knowledge of the truth (1 Tim. 2:4).

The Lord is not slow to fulfill his promise as some count slowness, but is patient toward you, not wishing that any should perish, but that all should reach repentance (2 Peter 3:9).

And Jesus said, "Father, forgive them, for they know not what they do" (Luke 23:34).

People get it wrong and think it's about being good enough, when in reality it's about being lost and not knowing it. Jesus came on an all-out rescue mission to seek and save the lost—every sinner. He didn't come to partially save us and watch to see if we could qualify for heaven. He qualified the unqualified. He died for the ungodly, the sinner. The only way to not be saved is to reject the Truth (Jesus) right before your eyes.

What about those who have never heard of Jesus? I can't believe God would send someone to hell simply for not believing in Jesus.

It is true that some may not have heard of Jesus, but we've learned that the Bible says God is obvious to everyone through creation and their conscience. Consider if you were up in a plane and chose to jump out without putting on a parachute. The primary reason you would die is not because you failed to put on a parachute, it's because you violated the law of gravity. We have a similar situation with sin, since every person has violated God's law written on their conscience. Our acts of lawbreaking are the reason the Bible says we are under condemnation. Jesus is the Savior—a parachute that God is freely offering to save us from the condemnation of the law. If someone declines to put on the parachute, that's their choice, not God's.

When we consider those who have never heard of Jesus or the gospel message, this is one of those places where we need to let faith step in. We know that God's nature is the pinnacle of morality as displayed in Jesus' life and teachings. We can also see His unconditional love for us displayed in the ultimate sacrifice He made to save us. Therefore, Christians, by faith, believe God will deal with anyone that does not hear of Jesus in the fairest manner possible.

In addition, the Bible indicates that young children who die go to heaven. In addition, there are recent reports from the Middle East that fifty percent of the Muslims who are turning to Christ are coming because of dreams and visions, indicating that God can reach people anywhere.

Another possibility suggested by Dr. William Lane Craig of reasonablefaith.org is that those who never hear could have been placed where they are by God because He knew they would reject Him even if they did hear. Since you are not one of those who have not heard, the best thing you can do is get right with God and then go and tell someone.

Read about a third possibility. Just Google: Michael Edwards New Covenant Bible Studies - What About Those Who Never Hear of Jesus or the Gospel

The Fall of Man

To further amplify everyone's need for Jesus as Savior, I want to point out how exacting God's law is when it comes to sin. The general description of humanity's descent into sin is called the fall of man. I like to compare the situation to the law of gravity, where it only takes one step off the edge of a cliff to begin the fall to your death. God's natural laws, like gravity, were established for the greater good, but they do not respect individuals—we must respect them. It makes sense that the same would be true with God's moral law, which the Bible calls the law of sin and death. The Bible says it only took one sin for us to step off the cliff of perfect morality and find ourselves falling, with no hope of saving ourselves.

For whoever keeps the whole law but fails in one point has become accountable for all of it (James 2:10, emphasis added).

Although this sounds harsh, it means it only took one sin to separate us from God. He provides this warning for our benefit so we will take action and seek the solution. The main themes of the Bible are God's holiness, our sinfulness, and God's plan to save us. He loves you, and the only way He can save you is with your cooperation. The only way you will cooperate is to understand and accept the truth of your sinful condition.

"But as for the cowardly, the faithless, the detestable, as for murderers, the sexually immoral, sorcerers, idolaters, and all liars, their portion will be in the lake that burns with fire and sulfur, which is the second death" (Rev. 21:8, emphasis added).

The Bible is crystal clear. Even if you have led a completely sacrificial life doing good for others like Mother Theresa, you still fall short of God's perfect standard. You need to repent (change your mind) and trust in Jesus by accepting the payment He made for our sins on the cross. Those who do not will be required to pay for their own sins, eternally separated from God.

The Bible says that Jesus came to justify us—to make us right with God. To maintain that you are good enough is self-justification. It's telling God that you do not need His help. He can only help you when you admit you cannot help yourself and call to Him.

For we hold that one is justified by faith apart from works of the law (Rom. 3:28).

Faith Steps into the Picture

Remember my analogy of walking across the ice to the other side of a frozen lake? Before we started to cross, we checked out the facts as best we could. But eventually, we needed to add faith to what we had discovered if we wanted to get to the other side. That's where we stand now with God and the Bible. The evidence has given us answers to many questions and, up to this point, the Bible and God have checked out. We have verified truths about Jesus and now we need to decide if we want to trust Him with the things He claimed, which cannot be verified. This is where faith needs to take over.

Knowing the Bible says you are headed to hell doesn't sound like a blessing at first, but think of it this way—if you had a deadly but curable disease and did not know it, you would never seek a cure. But once you have the diagnosis, the fear of death would motivate you to set aside everything else to seek a doctor with the cure. When you found him, you would need to heed his advice to survive. In the same way, let the diagnosis of your sinful condition motivate you to set aside any distractions. Listen to God, who loves and cares for you and has the cure for your condition—the good news that Jesus paid for your sins on the cross. It's the ultimate proof and an undeniable testimony that God loves you and wants to save you.

For while we were still weak, at the right time Christ died for the ungodly. For one will scarcely die for a righteous person—though perhaps for a good person one would dare even to die. but God shows his love for us in that while we were still sinners, Christ died for us (Rom. 5:6-8).

We do not place our faith and trust in Jesus primarily for a better life. We trust in Him to make us righteous: right with God. It's the —Great Exchangell in which Jesus freely exchanges His righteousness for our sinfulness.

Have You Met Grace?

When we discover our guilt before God, our first reaction might be to try to fix ourselves by doing better. But think of a man who committed numerous crimes and wasn't caught for years. He knows what he did was wrong, so he reforms his life. One day, years later, there is a knock on the door—it's the police. The law has caught up with him and even though he has reformed, his crimes must still be punished. We see a clear example of this with

Nazi war criminals who are still being arrested and prosecuted today, after years of hiding. The same is true with all of the numerous sins we have already committed. The Bible says they cannot go unpunished and good deeds now, while well-intentioned, are not the answer. The Bible offers an amazing solution: the gift of salvation by grace, God's undeserved favor.

Grace alone is crucially important to grasp, and Biblical Christianity is the only belief in God that claims that salvation is by grace through faith alone. The next verse teaches that the only way we can be saved is by the grace of God.

For by grace you have been saved through faith. And this is not your own doing; it is the gift of God, not a result of works, so that no one may boast (Eph. 2:8-9, emphasis added).

If you went to work, did nothing and still got paid, that's grace. Grace and works are contradictory, as the apostle Paul points this out in the next verse:

But if it is by grace, it is no longer on the basis of works; otherwise grace would no longer be grace (Rom. 11:6).

For Christ is the end of the law for righteousness to everyone who believes. Rom 10:4

For sin will have no dominion over you, since you are not under law but under grace. Rom 6:14

In the following verse, Paul tells us if we could earn our righteousness, right standing with God, and thus entrance into heaven by doing good, Christ died for nothing.

I do not nullify the grace of God, for if righteousness were through the law, then Christ died for no purpose (Gal. 2:21).

Lastly, a clear example of salvation by grace alone can be seen in a conversation between Jesus and the two thieves crucified on the crosses next to Him. The first part of the dialogue is between the two thieves, one humble and one rebellious unto death. The second part, quoted here, is when the humble thief turns to Christ, admits his guilt and places his faith in Him.

But the other rebuked him, saying, "Do you not fear God, since you are under the same sentence of condemnation? And we indeed justly, for we are receiving the due reward of our deeds; but this man (Jesus) has done nothing wrong" (Luke 23:40-41).

And he said, "Jesus, remember me when you come into your kingdom." And he (Jesus) said to him, "Truly, I say to you, today you will be with me in paradise" (Luke 23:42-43, emphasis added).

Obviously, the thief who humbled himself and threw himself on God's mercy could not accomplish any good works before he died, yet Jesus said, "Today you will be with me in paradise." Here are a few more of the numerous verses that teach salvation by grace alone: Romans 3:28-30; 4:5; 5:1; 9:30; 10:4; Galatians 2:16; 2:21; 3:5-6; 3:24; Ephesians 2:8-9.

Grasping grace alone can be tough. Therefore, let me end this subject on a personal note that might help. I too struggled with the thought there must be something I needed to do. Finally, I decided to do the only thing I could—take God at His Word. I accepted that I could never be good enough based on God's standard, and it is impossible to earn a gift. If salvation is a gift as the Bible promises, the only option anyone has is to trust God and accept it. The burden to keep the promise is always on the promise maker. In this case, the promise maker is God. We know he is powerful enough to fulfill His promise and the Bible tells us God cannot lie. So, we have the best promise maker that exists.

—I CANNOT get to Heaven on the basis of anything that I have done. I need to come to God with an open heart and confess that it is not because of who I am, but because of what He's done; not because of what I've done, but because of who He is. God Alone. Faith Alone. Anything else would be an insult to the Giver of Life.‖ Jim Wallace, former atheist, homicide detective, www.pleaseconvinceme.com

Grace is Not an Excuse

The Bible says that we need Jesus to save us from God's wrath towards sin—this confirms that God's law is good and endures. Paul preached grace, yet he often had to instruct believers that grace is not a license to sin.

What then? Are we to sin because we are not under law but under grace? By no means! (Rom. 6:15).

Although it's clear that the Bible says good works cannot save anyone, Jesus taught us to do good and our conscience confirms this is God's desire. A Christian's actions verify the reality of their faith, which is not visible apart from good works. So first, place your faith in Jesus, and then do good works out of gratitude because your salvation is guaranteed in Christ.

But someone will say, "You have faith and I have works." Show me your faith apart from your works, and I will show you my faith by my works (James 2:18, emphasis added).

—Good works are a fruit of our salvation, not a root of our salvation.‖ Andrew Womack, www.awmi.net

Small Town Judge

The Good Person test revealed our guilty condition before God. In John 14:6, Jesus discloses He is the only solution for our situation and the only way to the Father. The following analogy will clarify why Jesus' payment for our sins was necessary and He is the only way for mankind to be saved.

Imagine you live in a very small town where there is only one judge, who is also your father. He is an ethical judge who always enforces the law. You are his favorite child. You help family and friends whenever they need it, get top grades in college, hold down a good job to support your young family and give to charity. Then one night you go out with friends and drink too much. On your way home you're arrested for DUI and reckless driving. In one instant you are in big trouble with the law.

Your day in court arrives, and if found guilty you face the option of a $5,000 fine or six months in jail. Since your father is the only judge in town, you must stand before him. As he gazes down at you from the bench, imagine the awful dilemma you have placed him in. He loves you dearly, but he is an ethical judge, bound to uphold the law.

According to the Bible, God is in a similar position with us. He loves us dearly, but His just nature is fully aware of every wrong thought and action we have ever committed. He knows for certain that we are guilty.

Finally, your father offers his review of the evidence, indicates you are guilty and asks if you have anything to say for yourself. You say, —Dad, I know I am guilty, but I just messed up this one time. You know I am a good person.‖ You remind your dad of all the good things you have ever done and how this is the only mistake you've made. Then you begin to plead with him. —Dad, there are a lot of people much worse than me. I do not have the $5,000 for the fine, and if I go to jail, I will lose my job, get kicked out of school and my family will be destitute.‖ You pause, then blurt out: —Please overlook the law this one time and let me go.‖

The question is, can he do it and remain ethical? According to the thousands I have asked, the answer is a definite —NO.‖ They all agree that if he let you go, he would be corrupt.

The judge says, —Son, you know I love you dearly, but you also know I must uphold the law. I would be corrupt if I ignored it and let you go. I find you guilty as charged.‖ Somewhat in shock, you resign yourself to the thought that you are headed off to jail for six months. Then you notice your father standing at your side without his judge's robe, holding $5,000 in his hand. Amazingly, he is offering to pay your fine. You need to make a decision.

1. Reject the offer and pay for your crime in jail.

2. Accept the offer and go free.

No matter which choice you select, the law is fully satisfied and the judge remains ethical. He imposed the full penalty required by law, and now he offers to pay your fine. He found the only way to fulfill his love for you and to satisfy the law's requirement of justice at the same time.

This is a picture of what the Bible says God chose to do for humanity and why Jesus' payment on the cross for our sins is the only way to freedom. God's perfect moral nature requires all sin to be punished; God's loving nature wants to save you from that punishment. The only way God could possibly satisfy both of His natures was to pronounce our guilt, as His just nature requires, then take our punishment Himself, paying for our sins in full. He offers to freely exchange His righteousness for our sinfulness as a gift. A legal and binding transaction took place on the cross when the requirement of the law was fulfilled through Jesus' payment for our sins. Now you need to make a decision.

Perfect Justice collided with Perfect Love and Love won at the cross. Yes, God does forgive sins—but only for those who freely repent and place their faith entirely in Jesus, accepting the required payment He made on the cross. The only thing that stands in the way of your salvation is you. In this next verse God tells you which choice to make.

I call heaven and earth to witness against you today, that I have set before you life and death, blessing and curse. Therefore choose life, that you and your offspring may live (Deut. 30:19).

The Gravity of Your Decision

God cannot perform the logically impossible. He cannot make a one ended stick, a square circle, or please everyone's contradictory desires—for example, not everyone can be the richest, happiest or best looking person on earth. And He certainly cannot force a person with free will to accept His love, help, and salvation. Therefore, our free will holds unbelievable power. You need to decide if you want to trust God, who knows all things and loves you, or continue to trust your limited knowledge. The gravity of your decision is immense.

I realize that many face an internal struggle when they consider trusting Jesus. I feared the change I might need to make, and I feared that God did not love me. After all, He knew everything I had ever done. Initially, I believed the lies that Christianity was all about keeping a bunch of rules to appease an angry God and that I needed to clean up my life before God would accept me. I realize now I was just using that as an excuse to ignore God and continue in my ways. This is not about being perfect and forcing yourself to change by your willpower. It is about accepting the truth of our sinful condition and being willing to let God do for us what is impossible for us to do in our own strength.

Jesus came on an all-out rescue mission for us, not to judge us or see if we can keep the rules to qualify. He fully qualifies all who will trust in Him: for eternal life and to participate in the inheritance of the Saints.

The men and women described in the Bible were real people, just like you and me. They had emotions and feelings just as we do, and they stumbled and fell short at times as believers. You will not be an exception. But God will transform you from the inside out at His pace, with His power and your cooperation. I often do not sense that anything is happening. But when I look at myself now, even though I may not be where I would like to be, I am not where I used to be. Do not fear; come just as you are, no matter who you are or what you are doing or have done. Turn around and let Jesus save you now.

"He is no fool who gives what he cannot keep to gain that which he cannot lose." Jim Elliot, was killed sharing the gospel.

Upon accepting Christ, the Bible says our Spirit is immediately justified and made right with God. This justification is a one-time act of God in which He places us in a right relationship with Him, solely because of what Jesus accomplished on the cross. God then sees us in the Spirit in the perfection of Christ, just as if we had never sinned.

Then God, who loves us just as we are but wants more for us, begins His process of renewing our minds and thoughts to the truth of who we now are in Christ.

When we first trust Christ, we still have the same old computer program in our brain, filled with the same old thoughts. This can often lead to the same errors we have made for years, so we need to be patient and trust God. His process of renewal can take time to show up on the outside. It is all dependent on our level of cooperation. But no matter what, as soon as you trust Jesus, you are made right with God, saved from all condemnation and have inherited eternal life.

No Christian is better than anyone else, but like a person who accepts the evidence that the plane is going down and puts on the parachute, they are better off.

God's Talking—Are You Listening?

Listen to the still, small voice inside of you. Ask God if Jesus is the truth, then thoughtfully read the verses below. After each one, pause and consider what it says to you:

For all have sinned and fall short of the glory of God (Rom. 3:23).

For the wages of sin is death, but the free gift of God is eternal life in Christ Jesus our Lord (Rom. 6:23).

God shows his love for us in that while we were still sinners, Christ died for us (Rom.5:8).

Jesus said to him, "I am the way, and the truth, and the life. No one comes to the Father except through me" (John 14:6).

And there is salvation in no one else, for there is no other name under heaven given among men by which we must be saved. (Acts 4:12).

Jesus answered him, "Truly, truly, I say to you, unless one is born again he cannot see the kingdom of God" (John 3:3, emphasis added).

If you confess with your mouth that Jesus is Lord and believe in your heart that God raised him from the dead, you will be saved. For with the heart one believes and is justified, and with the mouth one confesses and is saved. For the Scripture says, "Everyone who believes in him will not be put to shame" (Rom.10:9-11).

Reasonable Faith

It's normal to still have questions and doubts, but that shouldn't keep you from deciding to trust Jesus. Remember, I never said the evidence would prove the Bible is true beyond all possible doubt; however, I believe the evidence indicates it is true beyond all reasonable doubt, like in a court of law. The only thing proven beyond all possible doubt is our guilt before a Holy God.

If our airplane was about to crash and I handed you a parachute, wouldn't you have fears about using it, even though you knew beyond a reasonable doubt that parachutes work? But if you trusted those fears and never put the parachute on, you would surely die. On the other hand, if you trusted what you did know about parachutes and put it on, you would most likely live. The same logic applies to God. You now know more about the facts than many Christians. I beg you to trust Jesus. He will never let you down.

"...he has said, "I will never leave you nor forsake you" (Heb. 13:5). "....And behold, I am with you always, to the end of the age" (Matt. 28:20).

You must freely repent, change your mind, believe the good news and turn to the one and only living God. Put on the Savior as you would a parachute, so you're ready for your jump into eternity.

If you desire to accept Jesus and to receive the salvation that He offers, but you do not know what to say, it's okay. The words are not as important as your heart. The Bible compares our relationship with God to a marriage in which we have been the unfaithful partner. Consider a person who has been unfaithful to their spouse, realizes the huge mistake they have made and wants to repair the damage. No one would need to tell them what to say. They would just cry out from their heart after coming to their senses, promising to turn from their wayward path while asking for forgiveness.

Do the same with God. Humble yourself, admit your sins and turn to God's saving grace. It does not matter who you are, your age, or what you have done. The apostle Paul, the author of the majority of the New Testament, was persecuting and killing Christians up until the very moment God saved him. Come just as you are. God will not reject a humble heart. Here is a short prayer to guide you:

—Lord God, I admit I am a sinner in desperate need of your saving grace. I believe Jesus Christ is God in the flesh and He died on the cross to pay the penalty for my sins in full. He then rose again and defeated death. I thank you and I accept your free gift of forgiveness, salvation and eternal life. I commit to following you, Lord Jesus. I pray for Your will, not mine to be done. Amen

You do not need anyone's help to trust Jesus, but if you have questions or feel led to talk to someone directly, call 1-800-NEEDHIM or visit www.chataboutjesus.com

If you have made a decision for Christ, welcome to God's family. I sincerely believe you have exercised reasonable faith based on the facts. I urge you to continue your study of the evidence by going to my website, www.god-evidence- truth.com and by Googling Michael Edwards New Covenant Bible Studies for many Bible studies I have written to help you in your walk.

You need to realize that Jesus is your only example and that God's power is in His Word. John 1:1 tells us, —In the beginning was the Word, and the Word was with God, and the Word was God‖ (emphasis added). To hear from God, you need to read the Bible. Start reading in the Gospel of John and ask God to help you understand, then read the other three Gospels and the rest of the New Testament.

Focus on studying the New Covenant of grace and truth that Christians are under exclusively. The New Covenant starts after the cross in the Bible. The book of Hebrews is all about the New Covenant that Jesus shed His blood to bring us. Think of it this way: if you had a rich uncle who left an old and a new will, which will would you want to see? Which will would apply to his inheritance? The new of course. The old would be obsolete and no longer apply. This same truth applies to the Old Covenant of law given by Moses. Jesus died to place into effect the New Covenant of grace and truth and we are co-heirs with Christ.. The old is based on the law and being able to keep God's standard perfectly and therefore deserving to be right with God. The new, on the other hand, is about grace: undeserved favor. We need Jesus because we cannot keep God's perfect standard, and this will never change in this life. The new replaced the old completely. Study the New Covenant and walk in it exclusively to walk in the power of the gospel.

And likewise the cup after they had eaten, saying, "This cup that is poured out for you is the new covenant in my blood." Luke 22:20

Under the New Covenant, you will learn that believers are placed under grace, no longer under the dominion of the law or condemnation in Gods eyes.

For sin will have no dominion over you, since you are not under law but under grace. Rom 6:14

You will also learn that you are totally forgiven for all sins for all time. God is not counting your sins: He sees your faith instead.

For I will be merciful toward their iniquities, and I will remember their sins no more." Heb 8:12

I have written hundreds of Bible studies on the New Covenant. Google: Michael Edwards New Covenant Bible studies.

Filter things you hear about God, Jesus and Salvation through the truth of the Word. Like a compass that always points north, let the Bible be your guide that always points to the truth. Know what it says, follow it and never get lost again.

While a person can be saved without going to church, I strongly suggest that you find a good Bible-believing church. Don't expect it to be perfect. If any church was perfect and any of us showed up, we would ruin it. In reality, church is for the believer, not God; it is a hospital for sinners, not a museum for saints. We go to church to encourage each others' faith. Find a small group Bible study and some like-minded, believing friends. I also find tremendous value in a good Christian radio station or Christian music that will feed your spirit and help to keep your thoughts on God.

If you have seen yourself in the light of God's truth, you will be able to intimately relate to the following lyrics written by the reformed slave trader John Newton. Compared to God, he could clearly see the wretchedness that dwelled within him, and therefore the amazing grace of God.

Amazing Grace, how sweet the sound, That saved a wretch like me. I once was lost but now am found, Was blind, but now I see. T'was Grace that taught my heart to fear. And Grace, my fears relieved. How precious did that Grace appear The hour I first believed. Through many dangers, toils and snares I have already come; 'Tis Grace that brought me safe thus far and Grace will lead me home. The Lord has promised good to me. His word my hope secures. He will my shield and portion be, As long as life endures. Yea, when this flesh and heart shall fail, And mortal life shall cease, I shall possess within the veil, A life of joy and peace. When we've been here ten thousand years Bright shining as the sun. We've no less days to sing God's praise Than when we've first begun.

Not sure yet? Critical points to remember

If you are unsure, I encourage you to candidly ask God if Jesus is the truth. Keep your eyes and ears open over the next couple of weeks, and He will confirm it for all who are sincere. But remember:

1. God's truth applies to you, whether you believe it or not.
2. God's standard is perfection.
3. We all fall short, and Jesus is our only hope.
4. Ten out of ten people die, so don't take too long to decide.

Please let me know if this book made a difference in your life and if you placed your faith in Jesus. It's not about religion, it's about truth. Enjoy the journey!

May God Richly Bless you, *Michael Edwards*

Full 40,000 word version of Gravity including more evidence can be found free online in an e-book at: God-Evidence-Truth.com. Google: Michael Edwards New Covenant Bible studies and my new book: Radical New Covenant Bible Studies by Michael Edwards.

Many thanks to Dr. Frank Turek and Dr. Norman Geisler for their book I Do Not Have Enough Faith to Be Atheist, Buy it at impactapologetics.com or Amazon.com.

Everyone deserves the chance to examine the facts and make a reasonable decision. Please pass this book on and tell others how they can get a free e-book version online at God-Evidence-Truth.com. Copies of this book can be ordered in ten packs on the site for a donation of roughly a $1 per copy.

Please pass this book on and get more to hand out. The FREE e-book version and print copies (at our cost) can be found online at god-evidence-truth.com.

I accepted Jesus as my Lord and Savior today. I know God always keeps His promises. I have been forgiven and have eternal life. Thank You, Father.

Decision for Christ

Name   **Date**

_____

_____

_____

_____

_____

_____

_____

40701767R00064